TEACHER'S EDITION

LEVEL 9

STECK-VAUGHN COMPANY
ELEMENTARY • SECONDARY • ADULT • LIBRARY

Acknowledgments

Executive Editor: Diane Sharpe
Project Editor: Janet Jerzycki
Editor: Amanda Johnson
Contributing Author: Jay Comras
Graphics Project Manager: Laura Cole
Graphics Assistant: Sheryl Bankford
Production: Go Media, Inc., Austin, Texas
Cover Design: D Childress/Alan Klemp
Illustrators: Sonya Cohen, Holly Cooper, Julie Gomoll, Rachel Matthews

Pronunciation key reproduced with permission of Macmillan/McGraw-Hill School Publishing Company from *Macmillan School Dictionary 1* (ISBN 0-02-195003-2) *Grade 3–5* and *Macmillan School Dictionary 2* (ISBN 0-02-195004-0) *Grade 6–8*. Copyright © 1990.

Test Best is a registered trademark of Steck-Vaughn Company.

Iowa Tests of Basic Skills is a trademark of The Riverside Publishing Company. Such company has neither endorsed nor authorized this test-preparation book.

ISBN 0-8114-2869-9
Copyright © 1995 Steck-Vaughn Company.
All rights reserved. No part of the material protected by this copyright may be reproduced or utilized in any form or by any means, electronic or mechanical, including photocopying, recording, or by any information storage and retrieval system, without permission in writing from the copyright owner. Requests for permission to make copies of any part of the work should be mailed to: Copyright Permissions, Steck-Vaughn Company, P.O. Box 26015, Austin, TX 78755.
Printed in the United States of America.

14 15 15 1409 13 12 11
4500281588

Contents

About the Program

est Best on the Iowa Tests of Basic Skills has been developed to fresh basic skills, familiarize students with test formats and rections, and to teach test-taking strategies for the Iowa Tests of asic Skills. Test Best provides teachers with materials to ensure at students take the test under optimal conditions—that test-wise udents be able to concentrate on what they know without being verwhelmed by a testing situation with which they are unfamiliar.

eing well prepared for a test means knowing how to approach fferent types of questions and how to use time wisely. By using the est Best books prior to the administration of the Iowa Tests of Basic kills, students will learn such skills, as well as be able to control eir anxiety about a test and to keep their concentration high roughout the testing period. Armed with the skills they have learned s they work through Test Best on the Iowa Tests of Basic Skills, udents can truly perform well.

he Steck-Vaughn Test Best Series for Grades K–8

est Best on the Iowa Tests of Basic Skills consists of nine student ooks. You will need to determine which book is best suited to the pilities and needs of your students. The series is organized as llows:

Book	Grade Level
Level 5	Kindergarten
Levels 6–7	Grade 1
Level 8	Grade 2
Level 9	Grade 3
Level 10	Grade 4
Level 11	Grade 5
Level 12	Grade 6
Level 13	Grade 7
Level 14	Grade 8

Objectives of the Series

To Increase Awareness of Test-Taking Strategies

Test-taking strategies should focus on three important test principles:
1. Time Use
   - Not spending too much time on any one question
   - Working rapidly but comfortably
   - Marking items to return to if time permits
   - Using any time remaining to review answers
   - Using a watch (at the appropriate age) to keep track of time
2. Error Avoidance
   - Paying careful attention to directions
   - Determining clearly what is being asked
   - Marking answers in the appropriate place
   - Checking all answers
   - Being neat by avoiding making stray marks on the answer sheet
3. Reasoning
   - Reading the entire question or passage and all the choices before answering a question
   - Applying what has been learned

To Increase Awareness of Directions

It is important that students understand the directions for taking the tests. Therefore, one of the key objectives of the program is to familiarize students with directions. Doing so builds self-confidence and permits students to utilize their time more effectively.

To Increase Awareness of Content and Skills

Anxiety often results from a lack of information about the knowledge and skills the tests will cover. You and your students will find that increased awareness of content and skills are significant outcomes of the program.

To Increase Awareness of Format

By practicing the skills needed to meet your school's educational objectives, the students will be gaining invaluable experience with test formats. Such familiarity permits students to spend more time applying what they have learned.

To Understand How the Test Is Administered

Students are sometimes uncomfortable anticipating what will happen on the day of the tests. Becoming familiar with the procedures, directions, and the process of test taking helps reduce anxiety and uncertainty.

Format of the Books

Each of the nine student books is divided into units that correspond to those found in the Iowa Tests of Basic Skills. The units vary but can include Vocabulary, Word Analysis, Listening, Reading Comprehension, Spelling, Language Mechanics, Language Expression, Math Concepts and Estimation, Math Problems, Math Computation, Maps and Diagrams, and Reference Materials. Within each of these units are the skills covered on the tests.

Each skill lesson generally includes
  Directions—clear, concise, and similar to those found in the Iowa Tests of Basic Skills;

Try This—a skill strategy for students that enables them to approach each lesson exercise in a logical manner;

A Sample—to familiarize students with test-taking items;

Think It Through—a specific explanation to students of the correct answer in the Sample item that tells why the incorrect answers are wrong and why the correct answer is correct;

A Practice Section—a set of exercises based on the lesson and modeled on the kinds of exercises found in the Iowa Tests of Basic Skills.

Each unit is followed by a Unit Test that covers all the skills in the unit lessons and affords students the opportunity to experience a situation close to the testing situation. Each book concludes with a series of Comprehensive Tests—one for each unit covered in the book. The Test Best Comprehensive Tests give students an opportunity to take a test under conditions that parallel those they will face when taking the Iowa Tests of Basic Skills.

The Teacher's Edition

The Teacher's Edition of Test Best on the Iowa Tests of Basic Skills contains a Scope and Sequence and reduced student pages complete with answers. The Teacher's Edition also provides a detailed plan of action and suggestions for teaching and administering each of the lessons and tests, including the Sample items. Scripts are provided so that students become familiar with the oral directions given on the tests themselves.

Also contained in the Teacher's Edition is an introductory lesson designed to acquaint students with the Test Best on the Iowa Tests of Basic Skills program. This lesson appears on pages 7 through 10 and should be used before beginning Lesson 1 with students.

Scope and Sequence

READING COMPREHENSION SKILLS

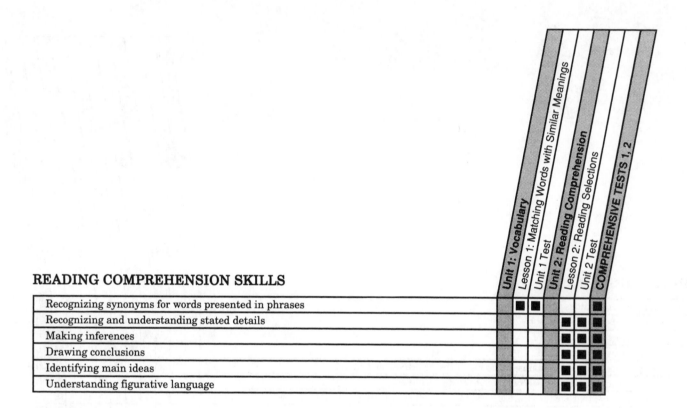

	Unit 1: Vocabulary	Lesson 1: Matching Words with Similar Meanings	Unit 1 Test	Unit 2: Reading Comprehension	Lesson 2: Reading Selections	Unit 2 Test	COMPREHENSIVE TESTS 1, 2
Recognizing synonyms for words presented in phrases		■	■				■
Recognizing and understanding stated details					■	■	■
Making inferences					■	■	■
Drawing conclusions					■	■	■
Identifying main ideas					■	■	■
Understanding figurative language					■	■	■

Scope and Sequence

LANGUAGE SKILLS

LANGUAGE SKILLS	Unit 3: Spelling	Lesson 3: Checking Word Spellings	Unit 3 Test	Unit 4: Language Skills	Lesson 4: Using Correct Capitalization	Lesson 5: Using Correct Punctuation	Lesson 6: Determining Usage	Lesson 7: Using Words Correctly	Lesson 8: Using Correct Expression	Lesson 9: Analyzing Paragraphs	Unit 4 Test	COMPREHENSIVE TESTS 3,4
Identifying correct spellings of words		■	■									■
Recognizing words spelled incorrectly		■	■									■
Recognizing errors in capitalization					■						■	■
Recognizing errors in punctuation						■					■	■
Recognizing errors in the use of nouns, pronouns, verbs, adjectives, and adverbs							■				■	■
Determining the appropriateness of conjunctions and verb forms								■			■	■
Identifying sentences that are the clearest, most correct, and most concise examples of effective writing									■		■	■
Determining the topic and supporting details of a paragraph										■	■	■
Determining sentence order in a paragraph										■	■	■

Scope and Sequence

MATHEMATICS SKILLS

MATHEMATICS SKILLS	Unit 5: Math Concepts and Estimation	Lesson 10: Working with Numeration	Lesson 11: Working with Number Sentences	Lesson 12: Using Measurement and Geometry	Lesson 13: Using Estimation	Unit 5 Test	Unit 6: Math Problems	Lesson 14: Solving Problems	Lesson 15: Working with Tables and Graphs	Unit 6 Test	Unit 7: Math Computation	Lesson 16: Adding	Lesson 17: Subtracting	Lesson 18: Multiplying	Lesson 19: Dividing	Unit 7 Test	COMPREHENSIVE TESTS 5, 6, 7
Understanding relative values of numbers		■				■											■
Recognizing different names for numbers		■				■											■
Understanding place value and expanded notation		■				■											■
Comparing and ordering numbers		■				■											■
Recognizing odd and even numbers		■				■											■
Understanding relative values of currency		■															■
Identifying fractional parts of sets		■															■
Understanding symbols for operations and relationships			■			■											■
Recognizing number sentences used to represent problems			■			■											■
Solving number sentences			■			■											■
Understanding number sentences used to represent number properties			■			■											■
Identifying appropriate units of measurement				■		■											■
Measuring quantity, time, length, and weight				■		■											■
Estimating measurements				■		■											■
Recognizing and comparing geometric figures				■		■											■
Determining perimeter and area of plane figures				■		■											■
Understanding spatial and geometric relationships				■		■											■
Rounding					■	■											■
Estimating					■	■											■
Solving one-step word problems								■		■							■
Solving multiple-step word problems								■		■							■
Distinguishing between necessary and extraneous data								■		■							■
Interpreting tables and graphs									■	■							■
Using data in graphic displays to solve problems									■	■							■
Horizontal and vertical addition of whole numbers												■				■	■
Horizontal and vertical subtraction of whole numbers													■			■	■
Horizontal and vertical multiplication of whole numbers														■		■	■
Division of whole numbers															■	■	■

STUDY SKILLS

Skill	Unit 8: Maps and Diagrams	Lesson 20: Working with Maps	Lesson 21: Working with Charts and Diagrams	Unit 8 Test	Unit 9: Reference Materials	Lesson 22: Alphabetizing	Lesson 23: Using a Table of Contents	Lesson 24: Using the Dictionary	Lesson 25: Using the Library	Unit 9 Test	COMPREHENSIVE TESTS 8, 9
Using standard map symbols and keys to describe and locate places	■	■									■
Determining direction and distance	■	■									■
Interpreting and drawing inferences from data	■	■									■
Using charts and diagrams to find information		■	■								■
Using charts and diagrams to determine relationships		■	■								■
Making inferences based on information in charts and diagrams		■	■								■
Comparing amounts in charts and diagrams		■	■								■
Alphabetizing words						■				■	■
Using a table of contents to locate information							■			■	■
Using a dictionary to determine spelling, pronunciation, and word meaning								■		■	■
Using a card catalog									■	■	■
Choosing appropriate reference materials to gather information									■	■	■

Introducing Students to *Test Best*

Use this orientation lesson to familiarize students with the format of *Test Best* on the *Iowa Tests of Basic Skills, Level 9,* and with steps for preparing for and taking the Iowa Tests of Basic Skills.

SAY: **At certain times during the school year, you may take one or more achievement tests. These tests show how well you are doing in certain subjects, compared to other students of your age group across the country.**

Discuss test taking and how students feel about taking standardized tests.

SAY: **Do you remember the last time you took achievement tests? Were you nervous? Were you worried? How did you feel when you finished the tests? Do you think you did your best on the tests?**

Point out to students that most people worry when they have to take a test. Explain that *Test Best* practice lessons and class discussions can help reduce anxiety and help increase confidence.

SAY: **Try not to worry about achievement tests. These tests will not affect your school grades. Instead, the achievement tests will tell you some interesting things about yourself—about the skills you have mastered and the skills you need to learn.**

Distribute the *Test Best* books to students. Tell students that *Test Best* will familiarize them with the kinds of questions on the Iowa Tests of Basic Skills and how it feels to take this kind of test.

SAY: **Some test items will be more difficult than others. Some material may be new to you. But that's all right. You will be given enough time to work on each test.**

Allow students to skim through the books for a minute or two.

SAY: **Now we will look at one of the lessons. Turn to Lesson 4 on page 16. Put your finger on the <u>Directions</u>. Who will read the <u>Directions</u>?**

Explain that each lesson begins with a set of <u>Directions</u>. Ask students why it is important to read and follow directions when taking tests.

UNIT 4 — Language Skills

Lesson 4: Using Correct Capitalization

Directions: Darken the circle for the line that has a capitalization error. Darken the circle for *No mistakes* if there is no error.

> **TRY THIS** First, read the sentence or sentences. Then look at each line for a word that should be capitalized or a word that should not be capitalized.

S1 A My family and I took a
    B boat ride on Lake Gaston
    C last saturday morning.
    D *(No mistakes)*

> **THINK IT THROUGH** The correct answer is <u>C</u> because line C contains an error. <u>Saturday</u> should be capitalized. It is a proper noun.

STOP

1 A The parade begins tomorrow
  B at two o'clock at the corner of
  C first street and Stone Avenue.
  D *(No mistakes)*

4 J Many pioneers who traveled
  K west across America had to
  L cross the smoky mountains.
  M *(No mistakes)*

2 J My friend ellen clark
  K is having a birthday party
  L at the pizza restaurant.
  M *(No mistakes)*

5 A Carl and i rode our bikes
  B to the park so we could meet
  C our friends at the playground.
  D *(No mistakes)*

3 A My mother went to the
  B store. she needed to buy
  C some milk and bread.
  D *(No mistakes)*

6 J School will close the last week
  K in May. Teachers and Students
  L will have a long vacation.
  M *(No mistakes)*

GO ON

Answers
S1 Ⓐ Ⓑ ● Ⓓ   2 ● Ⓚ Ⓛ Ⓜ   4 Ⓙ Ⓚ ● Ⓜ   6 Ⓙ ● Ⓛ Ⓜ
1 Ⓐ Ⓑ ● Ⓓ   3 Ⓐ ● Ⓒ Ⓓ   5 ● Ⓑ Ⓒ Ⓓ

16

UNIT 4 Language Skills

Lesson 4: Using Correct Capitalization

Directions: Darken the circle for the line that has a capitalization error. Darken the circle for *No mistakes* if there is no error.

TRY THIS	First, read the sentence or sentences. Then look at each line for a word that should be capitalized or a word that should not be capitalized.

S1   A   My family and I took a

    B   boat ride on Lake Gaston

    C   last saturday morning.

    D   *(No mistakes)*

THINK IT THROUGH	The correct answer is C because line C contains an error. Saturday should be capitalized. It is a proper noun.

STOP

1   A   The parade begins tomorrow

    B   at two o'clock at the corner of

    C   first street and Stone Avenue.

    D   *(No mistakes)*

2   J   My friend ellen clark

    K   is having a birthday party

    L   at the pizza restaurant.

    M   *(No mistakes)*

3   A   My mother went to the

    B   store. she needed to buy

    C   some milk and bread.

    D   *(No mistakes)*

4   J   Many pioneers who traveled

    K   west across America had to

    L   cross the smoky mountains.

    M   *(No mistakes)*

5   A   Carl and i rode our bikes

    B   to the park so we could meet

    C   our friends at the playground.

    D   *(No mistakes)*

6   J   School will close the last week

    K   in May. Teachers and Students

    L   will have a long vacation.

    M   *(No mistakes)*

GO ON

Level 9

Answers

S1 Ⓐ Ⓑ ● Ⓓ   2 ● Ⓚ Ⓛ Ⓜ   4 Ⓙ Ⓚ ● Ⓜ   6 Ⓙ ● Ⓛ Ⓜ

16   1 Ⓐ Ⓑ ● Ⓓ   3 Ⓐ ● Ⓒ Ⓓ   5 ● Ⓑ Ⓒ Ⓓ

SAY: **Find the Try This section. Let's read Try This together. Try This suggests a way to answer the questions. There are other ways to figure the answer to a question. Try This offers one way. Now look at the Sample, called S1, below Try This. We will always work through the Samples together before you work the practice exercises on your own.**

Copy the Sample onto the chalkboard. Work through the Sample orally with students, and demonstrate the proper way to darken the answer spaces. Explain to students the importance of filling the answer space, pressing firmly on the pencil to make a dark mark, and erasing any stray marks that might be picked up as answers by the scoring machines.

SAY: **Now find Think It Through. Who will volunteer to read this section? Think It Through is an explanation of the best answer. Think It Through usually explains why the other choices are wrong.**

Ask students if they have any questions about the lesson features up to this point.

SAY: **What do you see below Think It Through? (The word STOP) What should you do when you see the word STOP? (Stop what you are doing.)**

Tell students that they will see the word STOP throughout the lessons and on the Iowa Tests of Basic Skills. Explain that the word STOP tells students to stop what they are doing, put their pencils down, and wait for further instructions from the teacher.

SAY: **What do you see below Think It Through and the word STOP? (Numbered exercises) Each lesson has a practice section with exercises.**

What do you see at the bottom of the page? (The words GO ON) These words tell you to turn to the next page and continue working.

Explain to students that the words GO ON will appear in two-page lessons, in many unit tests, and in many Comprehensive Tests.

Unit 4 Test

S1
A In August Ling will fly to
B Taiwan. she will visit her
C grandparents for two weeks.
D *(No mistakes)*

STOP

S2
J Pam has a saltwater fish
K tank with sea horses in it.
L Would you like to see it
M *(No mistakes)*

STOP

S3
A Tim couldn't get into
B his house because he
C forgetted his key.
D *(No mistakes)*

STOP

For questions 1–7, darken the circle for the line that has a capitalization error. Darken the circle for *No mistakes* if there is no error.

1
A The city swimming pool
B on Beaver Lane closes
C in september for the winter.
D *(No mistakes)*

2
J We wear red, white, and blue
K clothes and wave the American
L flag on the fourth of july.
M *(No mistakes)*

3
A We need to go to the library
B to find some Information
C about Queen Elizabeth.
D *(No mistakes)*

4
J When I got home from school,
K I saw mr. Crew walking his
L dog through the neighborhood.
M *(No mistakes)*

5
A My mother always reminds
B me to wash my hands with
C soap and hot water before i eat.
D *(No mistakes)*

6
J Harry ordered a pizza but
K forgot to tell the driver to
L deliver it to 301 circle drive.
M *(No mistakes)*

7
A We have a pet lizard named
B Herman. We found him when
C we went to the colorado river.
D *(No mistakes)*

GO ON
Level 9

Answers
S1 Ⓐ ● Ⓒ Ⓓ   S3 Ⓐ Ⓑ ● Ⓓ   2 Ⓙ Ⓚ ● Ⓜ   4 Ⓙ ● Ⓛ Ⓜ   6 Ⓙ Ⓚ ● Ⓜ
S2 Ⓙ Ⓚ ● Ⓜ   1 Ⓐ Ⓑ ● Ⓓ   3 Ⓐ ● Ⓒ Ⓓ   5 Ⓐ Ⓑ ● Ⓓ   7 Ⓐ Ⓑ ● Ⓓ

27

Have students turn to the Unit 4 Test on page 27. Explain that there is a unit test at the end of each unit that gives students an opportunity to practice taking a test. Have students locate the Samples at the beginning of the test. Tell students that you will always work the Samples together as a class before they work the rest of the test. Explain that this test will include the skills practiced in the unit lessons.

Ask students if they have any questions about the lessons or the unit tests. Explain that at the end of the book there are Comprehensive Tests.

Test 4: Language Skills

S1
A During the summer there is a
B craft fair in our town on the third
C saturday of every month.
D *(No mistakes)*

STOP

S2
J Mrs. Kato has two dogs.
K Their names are Chip and Big.
L She walks them every day.
M *(No mistakes)*

STOP

S3
A We made these here pillows.
B The feathers came from my
C grandmother's geese.
D *(No mistakes)*

STOP

For questions 1–7, darken the circle for the line that has a capitalization error. Darken the circle for *No mistakes* if there is no error.

1
A Mother said that I could not
B play after school because i'm
C going to the doctor's office.
D *(No mistakes)*

2
J At the school plant sale,
K Masako bought an african
L violet for her math teacher.
M *(No mistakes)*

3
A Kevin has a big black dog that
B loves to swim in the lake.
C Kevin named his dog coal.
D *(No mistakes)*

4
J Terry wants to go camping
K in june. The park gets too
L crowded later in the summer.
M *(No mistakes)*

5
A 304 Great West Road
B clovis, NM 64132
C November 3, 1995
D *(No mistakes)*

6
J Dear Robert,
K Congratulations on winning
L your first fishing tournament.
M *(No mistakes)*

7
A I wish I could have been there!
B sincerely yours,
C Rodrigo
D *(No mistakes)*

GO ON

SAY: **Turn to page 75. Read the title at the top of the page.** (*Test 4: Language Skills*) **There are nine Comprehensive Tests—one test for each unit in the book. When we take the Comprehensive Tests, we will follow the test conditions that will be used during the Iowa Tests of Basic Skills. For examp[le] I will provide you with sharpened pencils and scratch paper [for] the mathematics problems. Also, each test will have a time limit. The Comprehensive Tests will give you a final chance t[o] apply the skills that you practiced in the lessons in *Test Bes[t]* before you take the Iowa Tests of Basic Skills.**

Ask students if they have any questions about the Comprehensive Tests.

SAY: **When you take the Iowa Tests of Basic Skills, you may feel a little nervous at first. Try to remember what you have learned in *Test Best* about taking tests. You will be able to use what you have learned in your classes, too. Then you should be ready to do your very best.**

────────── Lesson 1: Matching Words with Similar Meanings ──────────

Directions: Darken the circle for the word or words that have the <u>same</u> or <u>almost the same</u> meaning as the word in dark type.

> | TRY THIS | Choose your answer carefully. The other choices may seem correct if you do not think about the meaning of the word in dark type. |

S1 **Repair** the road

A follow

B fix

C find

D cross

> | THINK IT THROUGH | The correct answer is <u>B</u>. All four choices are things that complete the phrase about the road. But only <u>fix</u> has the same meaning as the word in dark type, <u>repair</u>. |

STOP

---

1 Silly **grin**

A laugh

B word

C game

D smile

2 **Arrange** a meeting

J record

K plan

L watch

M leave

3 **Pound** nails

A pull

B break

C hit

D weigh

4 To **mold** clay

J shape

K throw away

L cut

M hold

5 A heavy **jacket**

A socks

B rain

C load

D coat

6 **Assisted** the neighbor

J called

K saw

L met

M helped

STOP

Answers

Level 9

S1 Ⓐ ● Ⓒ Ⓓ   2 Ⓙ ● Ⓛ Ⓜ   4 ● Ⓚ Ⓛ Ⓜ   6 Ⓙ Ⓚ Ⓛ ●

1 Ⓐ Ⓑ Ⓒ ●   3 Ⓐ Ⓑ ● Ⓓ   5 Ⓐ Ⓑ Ⓒ ●

1

UNIT 1 Vocabulary

Lesson 1: Matching Words with Similar Meanings

Reading Skill: Recognizing synonyms for words presented in phrases

SAY: **Turn to Lesson 1, Matching Words with Similar Meanings, on page 1.**

Check to see that all students find Lesson 1.

SAY: **In Lesson 1 you will practice matching words that have the same or almost the same meaning.**

Read the <u>Directions</u> to students.

SAY: **Now look at Try This.**

Read <u>Try This</u> to students.

SAY: **Now look at S1. Read the phrase silently and study the word in dark type. Then read the four answer choices silently. Darken the circle for the answer choice that has the same or almost the same meaning as the word in dark type, *repair*.**

Allow students time to choose and mark their answer.

SAY: **Now look at Think It Through.**

Read <u>Think It Through</u> to students. Check to see that all students have filled in the correct answer space. Ask students if they have any questions.

SAY: **Now you will practice matching more words that have the same or almost the same meaning. Put your finger on number 1. Do numbers 1 through 6 just as we did S1. When you come to the word *STOP* at the bottom of the page, put your pencils down. You may now begin.**

Allow students time to choose and mark their answers.

Review the questions and answer choices with students. Discuss with the class why one answer is correct and the others are not correct. Also check to see that students have carefully filled in their answer spaces and have completely erased any stray marks.

S1 Preparing for the test

A writing

B getting ready

C looking

D waiting

STOP

For questions 1–7, darken the circle for the word or words that have the <u>same</u> or <u>almost the same</u> meaning as the word in dark type.

1 A **meadow** of flowers

A vase

B garden

C field

D store

2 **Swift** runner

J fast

K great

L slow

M careful

3 A **chilly** day

A warm

B windy

C nice

D cool

4 Important **guest**

J journey

K message

L visitor

M job

5 The **final** race

A first

B fast

C last

D only

6 A **brief** story

J short

K sad

L long

M funny

7 To **discover** the truth

A tell

B hide

C know

D find out

STOP

Level 9

Answers

S1 Ⓐ ● Ⓒ Ⓓ   **2** ● Ⓚ Ⓛ Ⓜ   **4** Ⓙ Ⓚ ● Ⓜ   **6** ● Ⓚ Ⓛ Ⓜ

2

1 Ⓐ Ⓑ ● Ⓓ   **3** Ⓐ Ⓑ Ⓒ ●   **5** Ⓐ Ⓑ ● Ⓓ   **7** Ⓐ Ⓑ Ⓒ ●

Unit 1 Test

SAY: **Turn to the Unit 1 Test on page 2.**

Check to see that all students find the Unit 1 Test.

SAY: **In this test you will use the vocabulary skills that we have practiced in this unit. Now look at S1. Which word has the same or almost the same meaning as the word in dark type? Darken the circle for the correct answer.**

Allow students time to choose and mark their answer.

SAY: **You should have darkened the circle for choice *B*. *Getting ready* has the same meaning as the word in dark type, *preparing*.**

Check to see that all students have filled in the correct answer space. Ask students if they have any questions.

SAY: **Now you will finish the test on your own. Read the directions carefully. Put your finger on number 1. Do numbers 1 through just as we did S1. Read the phrases and answer choices carefully. Then darken the circle for each correct answer. When you come to the word *STOP* at the bottom of the page, put your pencils down. You may now begin.**

Allow students time to choose and mark their answers.

SAY: **It is now time to stop. You have completed the Unit 1 Test. Make sure you have carefully filled in your answer spaces and have completely erased any stray marks. Then put your pencils down.**

After the test has been scored, review the questions and answer choices with students. If students are having difficulty, provide them with additional practice.

Lesson 2: Reading Selections

Directions: Read the story carefully. Then read each question. Darken the circle for the correct answer.

| TRY THIS | More than one answer choice may sound correct. Choose the answer that best goes with the story. |

S1 Mike and his father found a dog in the park. They brought him home. Mike placed an advertisement in the newspaper about finding the dog. Two days later the dog's owner came to get her dog.

How did the dog's owner find out that her dog was with Mike?

A She saw Mike with the dog.

B She read about it in the newspaper.

C Mike's father told her.

D She searched until she found her dog.

| THINK IT THROUGH | The correct answer is B. The third sentence tells you that Mike placed an advertisement in the newspaper. You can guess that the owner read about her dog. |

STOP

The Egyptians made statues of sphinxes to honor kings and queens. A sphinx has the head of a human and the body of a lion. The oldest and largest sphinx is the Great Sphinx. It was built in the desert near Giza, Egypt, thousands of years ago. At times the Great Sphinx has been buried by sand. Weather has worn away part of the stone. Today scientists are working on ways to save the Great Sphinx.

1 What is a sphinx?

A A pet

B A real animal

C A person

D A make-believe animal

2 What is the land like where the Great Sphinx stands?

J Snowy   L Rainy

K Dry   M Full of trees

GO ON

Answers
S1 Ⓐ ● Ⓒ Ⓓ   2 Ⓙ ● Ⓛ Ⓜ
1 Ⓐ Ⓑ Ⓒ ●

Level 9

3

UNIT 2 Reading Comprehension

Lesson 2: Reading Selections

Reading Skills: Recognizing and understanding stated details; making inferences; drawing conclusions; identifying main ideas; understanding figurative language

SAY: **Turn to Lesson 2, Reading Selections, on page 3.**

Check to see that all students find Lesson 2.

SAY: **In Lesson 2 you will answer questions about selections that you read.**

Read the Directions to students.

SAY: **Now look at Try This.**

Read Try This to students.

SAY: **Now look at S1. Read the selection silently. Then answer the question that follows. How did the dog's owner find out that her dog was with Mike? Darken the circle for the correct answer.**

Allow students time to choose and mark their answer.

SAY: **Now look at Think It Through.**

Read Think It Through to students. Check to see that all students have filled in the correct answer space. Ask students if they have any questions.

SAY: **Now you will practice answering more questions about selections that you read. Read each selection carefully and answer the questions that follow it. Put your finger on number 1. Do numbers 1 through 20 just as we did S1. When you come to the words GO ON at the bottom of a page, continue working on the next page. When you come to the word STOP at the bottom of page 8, put your pencils down. You may now begin.**

Allow students time to choose and mark their answers.

"What a great day for a walk!" Sam said. He could hear the birds singing. Sam was glad he had made this trip to the mountains. After breakfast Sam took off, whistling a tune. His trail went up the mountain. He walked for a while, and then he looked for a rock to rest on. Sam was tired. "What a mountain man I turned out to be!" he said.

While he rested, Sam looked around. Suddenly he saw the opening to a cave. It was big enough to walk through. "I wonder how deep it is," he said. "I wonder if there are any cave drawings! I guess the only way to find out is to see for myself."

At first Sam had no trouble seeing in the cave. He went around a bend. He lit a match. "Just a little farther," he said to himself. Suddenly his match went out! He lit another one. But now things looked strange. Sam was lost!

When his second match went out, Sam got really frightened. Then he thought he heard a scratching noise. Sam struck his last match. In the light he saw hundreds of bats hanging on the cave walls! Their eyes glittered red. Sam started screaming and running as fast as he could. Luckily for Sam, he was running in the right direction. He ran all the way back to his camp.

GO ON

Level 9

3 What did Sam hear when he started his walk?

A Water running

B Mountain lions roaring

C Birds singing

D Bats scratching

4 What did Sam mean when he said, "What a mountain man I turned out to be"?

J He could not climb for as long as a real mountain man.

K He was not afraid of bats.

L He did not feel tired at all.

M He had decided to live on the mountain.

5 The opening to the cave

A was about four or five feet high.

B was less than one foot tall.

C had been blocked.

D led to cave drawings.

6 Sam was tired

J before breakfast.

K after he walked.

L when he lit his first match.

M when he saw the bats.

7 Why did Sam go into the cave?

A He was tired.

B He liked caves.

C He was a curious person.

D He was looking for a friend.

8 How did Sam feel when he saw the bats?

J Relieved

K Curious

L Angry

M Terrified

9 What is this story mainly about?

A Bats hanging on cave walls

B An adventure Sam had

C Using matches wisely

D Learning to be a mountain man

10 What is the meaning of the word "glittered" in the last paragraph?

J Blinked

K Saw

L Went out

M Shone

GO ON

Answers

3 Ⓐ Ⓑ ● Ⓓ   5 ● Ⓑ Ⓒ Ⓓ   7 Ⓐ Ⓑ ● Ⓓ   9 Ⓐ ● Ⓒ Ⓓ

4 ● Ⓚ Ⓛ Ⓜ   6 Ⓙ ● Ⓛ Ⓜ   8 Ⓙ Ⓚ Ⓛ ●   10 Ⓙ Ⓚ Ⓛ ●

Juana had just moved into a new house with her parents. She wanted to get a dog, and her parents finally agreed. Juana promised to walk the dog every morning before school. Every evening she would feed and brush it.

Her mother told her that she must get a small dog, since their new house and yard were not very big. But a small dog could still bark. It could warn them if someone was trying to break into the house.

On Saturday morning the family drove to the animal shelter. They looked at the dogs who needed homes. Juana fell in love with Shadow. She was a young black dog. She had big sad eyes and long, floppy ears. She seemed friendly and healthy. Mr. and Mrs. Ramirez liked her, too. Juana was very excited. She wanted to take Shadow home right then. But she would have to wait another day. The animal doctor needed to examine Shadow.

The family went home without Shadow. They came back the next day. The animal doctor found that Shadow was in fine health. He gave her all her shots. This time Juana went home with her new pet.

11 Why did the family members choose a small dog?

A It was the healthiest.

B Their house and yard were small.

C They were afraid of big dogs.

D They liked small dogs.

12 When did Shadow get her shots?

J Before the family first saw her

K When the animal doctor examined her

L When she was born

M The day she arrived at the shelter

13 What is this story mainly about?

A Animal shelters

B How to get a new pet

C How Juana gets a dog

D Shadow's shots

GO ON

Answers

11 Ⓐ ● Ⓒ Ⓓ   13 Ⓐ Ⓑ ● Ⓓ

6

12 Ⓙ ● Ⓛ Ⓜ

Did you know that whales are not really fish? They look like fish, and they live in the water. But they are not fish. They are mammals, just like dogs and people.

Most fish lay eggs and do not feed their young. Whales, however, give birth to live young. The babies are fed on their mother's milk. Fish use gills for breathing. Gills let them get oxygen from the water. Whales have lungs. They come to the top of the water from time to time to get oxygen from the air. Also, most fish are cold-blooded. This means that their body temperature changes with the surrounding temperature. Whales and other mammals are warm-blooded. This means that their body temperature stays the same when the surrounding temperature changes.

Many kinds of whales swim together in herds. Others live in family groups. Whales talk to each other by using different sounds. In this way they communicate over many miles.

People have always hunted whales for their oil. People in a few countries eat whale meat. Today certain kinds of whales are dying out. Some countries have stopped hunting whales in order to protect them.

14 **How are whales different from people?**

   J They are mammals.

   K They breathe oxygen.

   L They live in water.

   M They are cold-blooded.

15 **Why do whales make sounds?**

   A To communicate with other whales

   B Because they like the sounds

   C To communicate with other fish

   D To help them breathe

16 **What do a whale's lungs do?**

   J Get oxygen from the water

   K Keep the body temperature the same

   L Make sounds to communicate

   M Get oxygen from the air

17 **Why do some countries protect whales?**

   A Because they are like people

   B Because they live in family groups

   C So they will not die out

   D So they can swim in the water

GO ON

Answers
14 ⒥ ⓚ ● ⓜ   16 ⒥ ⓚ ⓛ ●
15 ● Ⓑ ⒸⒹ   17 ⒶⒷ ● Ⓓ

Review the questions and answer choices with students. Discuss with the class why one answer is correct and the others are not correct. Also check to see that students have carefully filled in their answer spaces and have completely erased any stray marks.

(a poem)

Perched on my hand
A trusting butterfly rested
Then spread its wings
To show me a flying flower.

18 In this poem, what is the flying flower?

J A daisy

K A hand

L A bee

M A butterfly

19 Why is the butterfly "trusting"?

A It knows that the person will not hurt it.

B It knows that the flowers are blooming.

C It knows it can fly well.

D It knows that the person will not tell its secret.

20 Which picture shows the butterfly in this poem?

J

K

L

M

STOP

Answers

8

18 Ⓙ Ⓚ Ⓛ ●   20 Ⓙ Ⓚ ● Ⓜ

19 ● Ⓑ Ⓒ Ⓓ

S1 Tony slumped down in the bus seat. He leaned his head against the window and yawned. It had been a long day. He had taken three tests at school and then tried out for the soccer team. He was glad that tomorrow was Saturday.

How did Tony feel?

A Proud

B Tired

C Excited

D Lonely

STOP

For questions 1–13, darken the circle for the correct answer.

> Grandma has told me many stories about what it was like growing up on the farm when she was a girl. Her family lived ten miles from any neighbors. They had little money to buy food in a store. They had to raise most of their food on the farm. They raised cows and chickens for meat. They grew and then canned fruits and vegetables to last the whole winter. Grandma's family stored some of the food in an underground cellar to keep it from spoiling. They also had an underground spring near the house. The water was very cold. They stored milk, butter, and eggs in the spring to keep them fresh.
>
> Grandma and her family had to work very hard. I am glad that we have cars and can go to the grocery store to buy our food.

1 Why did the grandmother's family grow much of their food?

A They could not afford to buy it.

B They wanted to make sure it was safe.

C There were no stores.

D The store did not have the kinds of food they liked.

2 How did the grandmother's family keep their milk and butter fresh?

J They canned it.

K They stored it in a spring.

L They used a refrigerator.

M They kept it in the cellar.

GO ON

Level 9

Answers
S1 Ⓐ ● Ⓒ Ⓓ   2 Ⓙ ● Ⓛ Ⓜ
1 ● Ⓑ Ⓒ Ⓓ

9

Unit 2 Test

SAY: **Turn to the Unit 2 Test on page 9.**

Check to see that all students find the Unit 2 Test.

SAY: **In this test you will use the reading skills that we have practiced in this unit. Look at S1. Read the selection silently. Then answer the question that follows. How did Tony feel? Darken the circle for the correct answer.**

Allow students time to choose and mark their answer.

SAY: **You should have darkened the circle for choice *B*. Tony took three tests and tried out for the soccer team. You can guess that he was *tired*.**

Check to see that all students have filled in the correct answer space. Ask students if they have any questions.

SAY: **Now you will finish the test on your own. Read the directions carefully. Now put your finger on number 1. Do numbers 1 through 13 just as we did S1. Darken the circle for each correct answer. When you come to the words *GO ON* at the bottom of a page, continue working on the next page. When you come to the word *STOP* at the bottom of page 12, put your pencils down. You may now begin.**

Allow students time to choose and mark their answers.

Many green plants are like food factories for humans. Lettuce, cabbage, and spinach have leaves that taste good. Some plant roots, like carrots, are a good source of food. One of our main food sources is the seed covering of plants. Did you know that fruits and vegetables are seed coverings? Squash and tomatoes contain seeds for new squash and tomato plants. Grapes, apples, peaches, and blueberries are delicious seed coverings. Sometimes we eat the plant seed itself. Walnuts and pecans are plant seeds. So are grains, such as rice, wheat, and oats. Beans, peas, and peanuts are also seeds.

3   **Which food is a leaf?**

A Tomato

B Lettuce

C Squash

D Carrot

4   **If you eat peanut butter, what part of the plant are you eating?**

J The seed

K The root

L The seed covering

M The leaves

5   **How are walnuts, oats, and peas alike?**

A They are all grains.

B They are all nuts.

C They are all seed coverings.

D They are all seeds.

6   **How are many plants like food factories for humans?**

J They need humans to work in them.

K They make food for humans to eat.

L They need a source of energy.

M They make seeds for new plants.

7   **What is this passage mainly about?**

A How to grow plants

B How plants give us food

C Different kinds of vegetables

D Seed coverings

GO ON

Level 9

Answers

3 Ⓐ ● Ⓒ Ⓓ   5 Ⓐ Ⓑ Ⓒ ●   7 Ⓐ ● Ⓒ Ⓓ

10

4 ● Ⓚ Ⓛ Ⓜ   6 Ⓙ ● Ⓛ Ⓜ

In this story a third-grade class is getting ready to have a Valentine's Day party.

Valentine's Day is not my favorite holiday. People get so mushy. But my mom had made a really neat cake for our party. It had little silver balls all over it. When you bit into them, they had chocolate inside.

Miss Andrews crooked her finger at me. "Andrea, your mother left a cake at the principal's office. Why don't you go get it?"

"My mother is bringing a cake, too. Can I go see if she left it?" The question came from Bernard.

Rudy snickered and I glared at him. Bernard always said his mother was bringing something for our parties. So far, she had not. But I guess Miss Andrews felt sorry for him, because she let him go with me.

When we got to the office, there was my mom's cake. I did fine until I tried to open the door and hold the cake too.

"Oh no!" cried Bernard. Splat! The cake landed on the floor, and some flew on the glass door. My face got hot. I was trying not to act like a baby and cry. That's when I saw a lady standing on the other side of the door. She had a big white box. Then I saw Bernard grinning from ear to ear.

I was lucky. My mom didn't get mad at me about the cake disaster. But I guess Bernard was even luckier. And you should have seen Rudy's face when Bernard opened the box!

8 **What did Andrea's mother put on her cake?**

J Red hearts

K Chocolate stars

L Silver balls

M Pink frosting

9 **Why did Miss Andrews send Andrea to the office?**

A She thought Andrea was rude to Rudy.

B She wanted Andrea to get the cake Bernard's mother left.

C She wanted Andrea to get the cake Andrea's mother left.

D She knew Andrea did not want to have a Valentine's Day party.

10 **Why did Bernard grin?**

J He wanted to be Andrea's friend.

K He thought Andrea's accident was funny.

L He was happy about the Valentine's Day party.

M He saw that his mother had brought a cake.

11 **Who is telling this story?**

A Bernard

B Rudy

C Andrea

D Miss Andrews

GO ON

Answers
8 Ⓙ Ⓚ ● Ⓜ   10 Ⓙ Ⓚ Ⓛ ●
9 Ⓐ Ⓑ ● Ⓓ   11 Ⓐ Ⓑ ● Ⓓ

Mother's Day was here, and Maurice wanted to get a special present for his mother. But he didn't have any money. Then he had an idea.

Maurice walked along the road and picked a beautiful bunch of wildflowers. He tied them with a red ribbon that his sister gave him. Then he gave them to his mother.

"Thank you, Maurice. They're beautiful," his mother said.

Maurice's mother smiled and gave him a big hug. She smelled the flowers. Suddenly she began to sneeze.

"Oh, Maurice, I like the flowers, but the flowers do not like me!" said his mother.

Maurice put his hands in his pockets and looked at the ground. What could he do now? Then he had another idea.

"Give the flowers to me, Mother. I know where to put them so you can look at them all the time," said Maurice.

He ran outside to the kitchen window. He put them on the window sill. Now Maurice's mother could enjoy the present.

12 What does Maurice's mother mean when she says, "But the flowers do not like me"?

J She knows that they are wildflowers.

K She does not like the flowers.

L The flowers make her sneeze.

M She likes the red ribbon.

13 Why did Maurice put the flowers on the window sill?

A Because they belonged outside

B To keep his mother from sneezing

C So his mother could smell them

D Because his mother did not like them

STOP

Level 9

Answers
12 Ⓙ Ⓚ ● Ⓜ
13 Ⓐ ● Ⓒ Ⓓ

12

After the test has been scored, review the questions and answer choices with students. If students are having difficulty, provide them with additional practice.

──────── Lesson 3: Checking Word Spellings ────────

Directions: Darken the circle for the word that is <u>not</u> spelled correctly. Darken the circle for *No mistakes* if there are <u>no</u> spelling errors.

TRY THIS	Look at each word carefully and say it silently to yourself. Decide which words you know are spelled correctly. Then look at the remaining words to make your choice.

S1 A come

B whine

C air

D play

E *(No mistakes)*

THINK IT THROUGH	The correct answer is <u>E</u>. There are no spelling mistakes in the answer choices.

STOP

1 A first
B meny
C will
D find
E *(No mistakes)*

2 J great
K little
L butter
M jelley
N *(No mistakes)*

3 A freeze
B before
C follow
D puzle
E *(No mistakes)*

4 J fans
K beachs
L toys
M listens
N *(No mistakes)*

5 A remane
B brightly
C jumped
D everyone
E *(No mistakes)*

6 J bottom
K bellong
L teach
M thirsty
N *(No mistakes)*

GO ON

Answers
Level 9

S1 Ⓐ Ⓑ Ⓒ Ⓓ ● 2 Ⓙ Ⓚ Ⓛ ● Ⓝ 4 Ⓙ ● Ⓛ Ⓜ Ⓝ 6 Ⓙ ● Ⓛ Ⓜ Ⓝ
1 Ⓐ ● Ⓒ Ⓓ Ⓔ 3 Ⓐ Ⓑ Ⓒ ● Ⓔ 5 ● Ⓑ Ⓒ Ⓓ Ⓔ

13

UNIT 3 Spelling

Lesson 3: Checking Word Spellings

Language Skills: Identifying correct spellings of words; recognizing words spelled incorrectly

SAY: **Turn to Lesson 3, Checking Word Spellings, on page 13.**

Check to see that all students find Lesson 3.

SAY: **In Lesson 3 you will practice finding words that have spelling mistakes.**

Read the <u>Directions</u> to students.

SAY: **Now look at Try This.**

Read <u>Try This</u> to students.

SAY: **Now look at S1. Read each answer choice carefully. Then darken the circle for the word that has a spelling mistake. Darken the circle for *No mistakes* if there is no spelling error.**

Allow students time to choose and mark their answer.

SAY: **Now look at Think It Through.**

Read <u>Think It Through</u> to students. Check to see that all students have filled in the correct answer space. Ask students if they have any questions.

7	A	about
	B	think
	C	beside
	D	evry
	E	*(No mistakes)*

8	J	sevin
	K	their
	L	bring
	M	oil
	N	*(No mistakes)*

9	A	walking
	B	needing
	C	stopping
	D	moving
	E	*(No mistakes)*

10	J	past
	K	voice
	L	tire
	M	notise
	N	*(No mistakes)*

11	A	which
	B	brocken
	C	family
	D	something
	E	*(No mistakes)*

12	J	field
	K	teach
	L	chain
	M	around
	N	*(No mistakes)*

13	A	circle
	B	steel
	C	travle
	D	hotel
	E	*(No mistakes)*

14	J	cover
	K	ghost
	L	flies
	M	smils
	N	*(No mistakes)*

STOP

Level 9

SAY: **Now you will practice finding more spelling mistakes. Put your finger on number 1. Do numbers 1 through 14 just as we did S1. When you come to the words *GO ON* at the bottom of the page, continue working on the next page. When you come to the word *STOP* at the bottom of page 14, put your pencils down. You may now begin.**

Allow students time to choose and mark their answers.

Review the questions and answer choices with students. Discuss with the class why one answer is correct and the others are not correct. Also check to see that students have carefully filled in their answer spaces and have completely erased any stray marks.

Answers

14

7 Ⓐ Ⓑ Ⓒ ● Ⓔ   9 Ⓐ Ⓑ Ⓒ Ⓓ ●   11 Ⓐ ● Ⓒ Ⓓ Ⓔ   13 Ⓐ Ⓑ ● Ⓓ Ⓔ

8 ● Ⓚ Ⓛ Ⓜ Ⓝ   10 Ⓙ Ⓚ Ⓛ ● Ⓝ   12 Ⓙ Ⓚ Ⓛ Ⓜ ●   14 Ⓙ Ⓚ Ⓛ ● Ⓝ

Unit 3 Test

S1	A	might	4	J	wellcome

S1 A might
    B those
    C thrugh
    D other
    E (No mistakes)

STOP

For questions 1–7, darken the circle for the word that is <u>not</u> spelled correctly. Darken the circle for *No mistakes* if there are <u>no</u> spelling errors.

1 A wirk
    B star
    C care
    D third
    E (No mistakes)

2 J howl
    K live
    L under
    M friend
    N (No mistakes)

3 A sail
    B afrade
    C space
    D clay
    E (No mistakes)

4 J wellcome
    K because
    L tease
    M today
    N (No mistakes)

5 A wooden
    B shown
    C elefant
    D complete
    E (No mistakes)

6 J spread
    K board
    L corner
    M erth
    N (No mistakes)

7 A brothers
    B surprise
    C choose
    D increas
    E (No mistakes)

STOP

Answers

S1 Ⓐ Ⓑ ● Ⓓ Ⓔ   2 Ⓙ Ⓚ Ⓛ Ⓜ ●   4 ● Ⓚ Ⓛ Ⓜ Ⓝ   6 Ⓙ Ⓚ Ⓛ ● Ⓝ
1 ● Ⓑ Ⓒ Ⓓ Ⓔ   3 Ⓐ ● Ⓒ Ⓓ Ⓔ   5 Ⓐ Ⓑ ● Ⓓ Ⓔ   7 Ⓐ Ⓑ Ⓒ ● Ⓔ

Unit 3 Test

SAY: **Turn to the Unit 3 Test on page 15.**

Check to see that all students find the Unit 3 Test.

SAY: **In this test you will use the language skills that we have practiced in this unit. Look at S1. Read the answer choices carefully. Then darken the circle for the word that has a spelling mistake. Darken the circle for *No mistakes* if there is no spelling error.**

Allow students time to choose and mark their answer.

SAY: **You should have darkened the circle for choice *C* because it shows a mistake in the spelling of *through*. The correct spelling is *t-h-r-o-u-g-h*.**

Check to see that all students have filled in the correct answer space. Ask students if they have any questions.

SAY: **Now you will finish the test on your own. Read the directions carefully. Put your finger on number 1. Do numbers 1 through 7 just as we did S1. Darken the circle for each correct answer. When you come to the word *STOP* at the bottom of the page, put your pencils down. You may now begin.**

Allow students time to choose and mark their answers.

SAY: **It is now time to stop. You have completed the Unit 3 Test. Make sure you have carefully filled in your answer spaces and have completely erased any stray marks. Then put your pencils down.**

After the test has been scored, review the questions and answer choices with students. If students are having difficulty, provide them with additional practice.

UNIT 4 Language Skills

Lesson 4: Using Correct Capitalization

Directions: Darken the circle for the line that has a capitalization error. Darken the circle for *No mistakes* if there is no error.

TRY THIS
First, read the sentence or sentences. Then look at each line for a word that should be capitalized or a word that should not be capitalized.

S1
- A My family and I took a
- B boat ride on Lake Gaston
- C last saturday morning.
- D *(No mistakes)*

THINK IT THROUGH
The correct answer is C because line C contains an error. Saturday should be capitalized. It is a proper noun.

STOP

1
- A The parade begins tomorrow
- B at two o'clock at the corner of
- C first street and Stone Avenue.
- D *(No mistakes)*

4
- J Many pioneers who traveled
- K west across America had to
- L cross the smoky mountains.
- M *(No mistakes)*

2
- J My friend ellen clark
- K is having a birthday party
- L at the pizza restaurant.
- M *(No mistakes)*

5
- A Carl and i rode our bikes
- B to the park so we could meet
- C our friends at the playground.
- D *(No mistakes)*

3
- A My mother went to the
- B store. she needed to buy
- C some milk and bread.
- D *(No mistakes)*

6
- J School will close the last week
- K in May. Teachers and Students
- L will have a long vacation.
- M *(No mistakes)*

GO ON

Level 9

Answers

S1 Ⓐ Ⓑ ● Ⓓ   2 ● Ⓚ Ⓛ Ⓜ   4 Ⓙ Ⓚ ● Ⓜ   6 Ⓙ ● Ⓛ Ⓜ
16   1 Ⓐ Ⓑ ● Ⓓ   3 Ⓐ ● Ⓒ Ⓓ   5 ● Ⓑ Ⓒ Ⓓ

UNIT 4 Language Skills

Lesson 4: Using Correct Capitalization

Language Skill: Recognizing errors in capitalization

SAY: **Turn to Lesson 4, Using Correct Capitalization, on page 16.**

Check to see that all students find Lesson 4.

SAY: **In Lesson 4 you will practice finding errors in capitalization.**

Read the Directions to students.

SAY: **Now look at Try This.**

Read Try This to students.

SAY: **Now look at S1. Read the sentence. Then darken the circle for the line that has an error in capitalization. Darken the circle for *No mistakes* if there is no error.**

Allow students time to choose and mark their answer.

SAY: **Now look at Think It Through.**

Read Think It Through to students. Check to see that all students have filled in the correct answer space. Ask students if they have any questions.

7 A   57 Skillman lane
   B   Weston, CT 06883
   C   June 18, 1995
   D *(No mistakes)*

8 J   dear Uncle Shelby,
   K   We are not able to
   L   visit you on Tuesday.
   M *(No mistakes)*

9 A Thank you for inviting us.
   B   your nephew,
   C   Brian
   D *(No mistakes)*

10 J Paul and Amy will fly to
   K Florida next week and spend
   L labor day with their aunt.
   M *(No mistakes)*

11 A Chan cooked a special dinner
   B for his family. He even baked
   C an Apple pie for dessert.
   D *(No mistakes)*

12 J Before we went to Mexico, we
   K took spanish lessons so we
   L could talk to the people there.
   M *(No mistakes)*

13 A Lindsay takes riding lessons
   B each week and rides a big
   C white horse named john.
   D *(No mistakes)*

14 J Please call Sharon and
   K tell her that i'm going
   L to be ten minutes late.
   M *(No mistakes)*

15 A Will you please repair the
   B window now? someone might
   C get hurt on the broken glass.
   D *(No mistakes)*

16 J When my dad was nine years
   K old, he wrote a letter each
   L week to a pen pal in England.
   M *(No mistakes)*

STOP
Level 9

Answers

| 7 ● Ⓑ Ⓒ Ⓓ | 9 Ⓐ ● Ⓒ Ⓓ | 11 Ⓐ Ⓑ ● Ⓓ | 13 Ⓐ Ⓑ ● Ⓓ | 15 Ⓐ ● Ⓒ Ⓓ |
| 8 ● Ⓚ Ⓛ Ⓜ | 10 Ⓙ Ⓚ ● Ⓜ | 12 Ⓙ ● Ⓛ Ⓜ | 14 Ⓙ ● Ⓛ Ⓜ | 16 Ⓙ Ⓚ Ⓛ ● |

17

SAY: **Now you will practice finding more errors in capitalization. Put your finger on number 1. Do numbers 1 through 16 just as we did S1. When you come to the words *GO ON* at the bottom of the page, continue working on the next page. When you come to the word *STOP* at the bottom of page 17, put your pencils down. You may now begin.**

Allow students time to choose and mark their answers.

Review the questions and answer choices with students. Discuss with the class why one answer is correct and the others are not correct. Also check to see that students have carefully filled in their answer spaces and have completely erased any stray marks.

Lesson 5: Using Correct Punctuation

Directions: Darken the circle for the line that has a punctuation error. Darken the circle for *No mistakes* if there is no error.

TRY THIS

First, read the sentence or sentences. Then look at each line to see if there is a missing punctuation mark or wrong punctuation.

S1 A The baby kicked his

B feet in the bathtub

C and giggled happily

D *(No mistakes)*

THINK IT THROUGH

The correct answer is C. Line C has a punctuation error because the sentence should end with a period.

STOP

---

1 A The children leave the house

B every morning at 715 so that

C they will not miss the bus.

D *(No mistakes)*

2 J My grandfather is coming

K to visit. I want to take him to.

L see the lion cubs at the zoo.

M *(No mistakes)*

3 A Mr. Chan gave a speech

B at the men's garden club

C luncheon on July 2 1995.

D *(No mistakes)*

4 J Carols radio was so loud

K that she did not hear the

L telephone when it rang.

M *(No mistakes)*

5 A Holly entered an art contest

B and won first prize Was she

C surprised when she found out!

D *(No mistakes)*

6 J The crane lifted the heavy

K boxes of bananas onto the

L ship in less than an hour.

M *(No mistakes)*

GO ON
Level 9

Answers

S1 Ⓐ Ⓑ ● Ⓓ   2 Ⓙ ● Ⓛ Ⓜ   4 ● Ⓚ Ⓛ Ⓜ   6 Ⓙ Ⓚ Ⓛ ●

18   1 Ⓐ ● Ⓒ Ⓓ   3 Ⓐ Ⓑ ● Ⓓ   5 Ⓐ ● Ⓒ Ⓓ

28   Level 9

Lesson 5: Using Correct Punctuation

Language Skill: Recognizing errors in punctuation

SAY: **Turn to Lesson 5, Using Correct Punctuation, on page 18.**

Check to see that all students find Lesson 5.

SAY: **In Lesson 5 you will practice finding errors in punctuation.**

Read the Directions to students.

SAY: **Now look at Try This.**

Read Try This to students.

SAY: **Now look at S1. Read the sentence. Then darken the circle for the line that has an error in punctuation. Darken the circle for *No mistakes* if there is no error.**

Allow students time to choose and mark their answer.

SAY: **Now look at Think It Through.**

Read Think It Through to students. Check to see that all students have filled in the correct answer space. Ask students if they have any questions.

7
A   409 Pine Street
B   Raleigh, NC 27612
C   May 22, 1995
D *(No mistakes)*

8
J   Dear Noriko
K   Thank you for the hat.
L   It was a great birthday present.
M *(No mistakes)*

9
A   Will you please write soon.
B   Your friend,
C   Missy
D *(No mistakes)*

10
J   Kay ate lunch in a restaurant.
K   She ordered a sandwich chips,
L   and a glass of milk.
M *(No mistakes)*

11
A   Mr. Holt watered his garden.
B   It had not rained for four days.
C   His flowers were wilting
D *(No mistakes)*

12
J   George Washington was born
K   on February 22 1732 in the
L   town of Wakefield, Virginia.
M *(No mistakes)*

13
A   Jenny bought two books and
B   a magazine, about France to
C   learn more about the country.
D *(No mistakes)*

14
J   Mrs Green will retire this year.
K   Did you know she has taught
L   school for twenty-two years?
M *(No mistakes)*

15
A   When Justin heard that
B   song. for the first time, he
C   didn't like it.
D *(No mistakes)*

16
J   My grandmother hadn't seen me
K   for three months. "You must visit
L   me more often," she said.
M *(No mistakes)*

STOP

Level 9

Answers

7 Ⓐ Ⓑ Ⓒ ●	9 ● Ⓑ Ⓒ Ⓓ	11 Ⓐ Ⓑ ● Ⓓ	13 Ⓐ ● Ⓒ Ⓓ	15 Ⓐ ● Ⓒ Ⓓ	
8 ● Ⓚ Ⓛ Ⓜ	10 Ⓙ ● Ⓛ Ⓜ	12 Ⓙ ● Ⓛ Ⓜ	14 ● Ⓚ Ⓛ Ⓜ	16 Ⓙ Ⓚ Ⓛ ●	**19**

SAY: **Now you will practice finding more errors in punctuation. Put your finger on number 1. Do numbers 1 through 16 just as we did S1. When you come to the words *GO ON* at the bottom of the page, continue working on the next page. When you come to the word *STOP* at the bottom of page 19, put your pencils down. You may now begin.**

Allow students time to choose and mark their answers.

Review the questions and answer choices with students. Discuss with the class why one answer is correct and the others are not correct. Also check to see that students have carefully filled in their answer spaces and have completely erased any stray marks.

Lesson 6: Determining Usage

Directions: Darken the circle for the line that has an error in the way the words are used. Darken the circle for *No mistakes* if there is no error.

TRY THIS

Read the sentence or sentences silently. Look at each line carefully. Listen for words or phrases that don't sound right.

S1 A Don't you wants to

B choose a kitten and

C take it home with you?

D *(No mistakes)*

THINK IT THROUGH

The correct answer is A. The word <u>wants</u> in line A is an error. <u>Want</u> is the correct verb for the subject of the sentence, <u>you</u>.

STOP

1 A Mrs. Top always sits on her

B front porch. She waves to all

C the childs as they walk by.

D *(No mistakes)*

2 J The stone house on the hill

K is the biggest house that

L Joseph has ever seened.

M *(No mistakes)*

3 A We usually get out

B of school early on the

C days that it snows.

D *(No mistakes)*

4 J There was a lot of food to

K eat at the picnic. Some of

L them pies were delicious.

M *(No mistakes)*

5 A On Saturday I and Ronnie

B went to the lake and fished.

C We caught four catfish.

D *(No mistakes)*

6 J That was the worstest pizza

K I have ever eaten. There was

L too much sauce on it.

M *(No mistakes)*

GO ON

Level 9

Answers

S1 ● Ⓑ Ⓒ Ⓓ   2 Ⓙ Ⓚ ● Ⓜ   4 Ⓙ Ⓚ ● Ⓜ   6 ● Ⓚ Ⓛ Ⓜ

20   1 Ⓐ Ⓑ ● Ⓓ   3 Ⓐ Ⓑ Ⓒ ●   5 ● Ⓑ Ⓒ Ⓓ

Lesson 6: Determining Usage

Language Skill: Recognizing errors in the use of nouns, pronouns, verbs, adjectives, and adverbs

SAY: **Turn to Lesson 6, Determining Usage, on page 20.**

Check to see that all students find Lesson 6.

SAY: **In Lesson 6 you will practice finding words that are used incorrectly.**

Read the <u>Directions</u> to students.

SAY: **Now look at <u>Try This</u>.**

Read <u>Try This</u> to students.

SAY: **Now look at S1. Read the sentence. Then darken the circle for the line that has an error in the way that the words are used. Darken the circle for *No mistakes* if there is no error.**

Allow students time to choose and mark their answer.

SAY: **Now look at <u>Think It Through</u>.**

Read <u>Think It Through</u> to students. Check to see that all students have filled in the correct answer space. Ask students if they have any questions.

7 A Fran was the hero of the game
   B when she ran to the wall
   C and catched the baseball.
   D *(No mistakes)*

8 J Dawn gots a lot of pets.
   K Last week her hamster
   L had seven babies.
   M *(No mistakes)*

9 A Our class went to the
   B zoo. We didn't see no
   C kangaroos or koala bears.
   D *(No mistakes)*

10 J Thomas and I finded an
   K old pair of sunglasses
   L by the swimming pool.
   M *(No mistakes)*

11 A Dan tried on a pair of shoes.
   B The shoes did not fit because
   C his feets were too big.
   D *(No mistakes)*

12 J Eve didn't go swimming
   K today because she didn't
   L wanna get her hair wet.
   M *(No mistakes)*

13 A Manny was having such
   B a good time that he didn't
   C want to leave the party.
   D *(No mistakes)*

14 J I gave my brother ten dollars
   K for his birthday. Him spent
   L it all playing video games.
   M *(No mistakes)*

15 A Terry was very thirsty. He
   B asked Mom for a glass of ice
   C water and dranked it quickly.
   D *(No mistakes)*

16 J Mr. and Mrs. Ito is going
   K to the school to watch
   L their son play basketball.
   M *(No mistakes)*

STOP

Level 9

Answers

7 Ⓐ Ⓑ ● Ⓓ   9 Ⓐ ● Ⓒ Ⓓ   11 Ⓐ Ⓑ ● Ⓓ   13 Ⓐ Ⓑ Ⓒ ●   15 Ⓐ Ⓑ ● Ⓓ
8 ● Ⓚ Ⓛ Ⓜ   10 ● Ⓚ Ⓛ Ⓜ   12 Ⓙ Ⓚ ● Ⓜ   14 Ⓙ ● Ⓛ Ⓜ   16 ● Ⓚ Ⓛ Ⓜ

21

SAY: **Now you will practice finding more words that are used incorrectly. Put your finger on number 1. Do numbers 1 through 16 just as we did S1. When you come to the words *GO ON* at the bottom of the page, continue working on the next page. When you come to the word *STOP* at the bottom of page 21, put your pencils down. You may now begin.**

Allow students time to choose and mark their answers.

Review the questions and answer choices with students. Discuss with the class why one answer is correct and the others are not correct. Also check to see that students have carefully filled in their answer spaces and have completely erased any stray marks.

Lesson 7: Using Words Correctly

Directions: Darken the circle for the word or words that will correct the underlined part of the sentence. Darken the circle for *No change* if there is no error.

TRY THIS	Read the sentence carefully. Think about the underlined word or words. After you choose your answer, read the sentence again, putting your answer in place of the underlined part.

S1   Carla **goes** to see a play yesterday.

   A has gone   B will go   C went   D *(No change)*

 THINK IT THROUGH   The correct answer is C. The word *yesterday* tells you that the events happened in the past. The past tense of *go* is *went*.

STOP

1   The two dogs ran **during** the ball.

   A in   B until   C after   D *(No change)*

2   When Grandfather visits, he **will tell** us stories.

   J told   K telling   L has told   M *(No change)*

3   After Dad took us to the fair, he **stop** to buy us some ice cream.

   A stopped   B will stop   C had stopped   D *(No change)*

4   I washed all the dishes **if** my mother took a nap.

   J whether   K than   L while   M *(No change)*

5   After we **will work** in the garden for an hour, we were hot and thirsty.

   A work   B had worked   C are working   D *(No change)*

6   Sandra started school **against** August 25, 1993.

   J in   K on   L from   M *(No change)*

STOP
Level 9

Answers
S1 Ⓐ Ⓑ ● Ⓓ   2 Ⓙ Ⓚ Ⓛ ●   4 Ⓙ Ⓚ ● Ⓜ   6 Ⓙ ● Ⓛ Ⓜ
22   1 Ⓐ Ⓑ ● Ⓓ   3 ● Ⓑ Ⓒ Ⓓ   5 Ⓐ ● Ⓒ Ⓓ

Lesson 7: Using Words Correctly

Language Skill: Determining the appropriateness of conjunctions and verb forms in sentences

SAY: **Turn to Lesson 7, Using Words Correctly, on page 22.**

Check to see that all students find Lesson 7.

SAY: **In Lesson 7 you will practice choosing the word or words that best fit in a sentence.**

Read the Directions to students.

SAY: **Now look at Try This.**

Read Try This to students.

SAY: **Now look at S1. Read the sentence silently. Then darken the circle for the word or words that will correct the underlined part of the sentence. Darken the circle for *No change* if there is no error.**

Allow students time to choose and mark their answer.

SAY: **Now look at Think It Through.**

Read Think It Through to students. Check to see that all students have filled in the correct answer space. Ask students if they have any questions.

SAY: **Now you will practice choosing more correct words. Put your finger on number 1. Do numbers 1 through 6 just as we did S1. When you come to the word *STOP* at the bottom of the page, put your pencils down. You may now begin.**

Allow students time to choose and mark their answers.

Review the questions and answer choices with students. Discuss with the class why one answer is correct and the others are not correct. Also check to see that students have carefully filled in their answer spaces and have completely erased any stray marks.

Lesson 8: Using Correct Expression

Directions: Darken the circle for the line that expresses the idea most clearly.

> **TRY THIS**
>
> Read each line carefully. Look for the sentence or sentences that are clear, well organized, and complete.

S1 A A beautiful picture painted. Nina wanted frame to it.

  B Nina painted a picture beautiful and to frame wanted it.

  C Wanted a frame to beautiful picture. Nina painted.

  D Nina painted a beautiful picture and wanted to frame it.

> **THINK IT THROUGH**
>
> The correct answer is D because it clearly expresses the idea. It is a clear, well-organized, complete sentence.

STOP

1 A Running so fast they wouldn't miss the bus.

  B Jed and Rusty ran fast so they wouldn't miss the bus.

  C Jed and Rusty running. So the school bus they wouldn't miss.

  D The school bus. Jed and Rusty running to it.

2 J Suki fell. The knee bike hurt her.

  K The knee fell on her bike and Suki hurt.

  L Off the bike fell Suki and hurt her knee.

  M Suki fell off the bike and hurt her knee.

3 A Tomorrow to the beach perhaps we'll go.

  B To the beach tomorrow. We'll go perhaps.

  C Perhaps we'll go to the beach tomorrow.

  D To the beach we'll go tomorrow perhaps.

GO ON

Answers

S1 Ⓐ Ⓑ Ⓒ ●   2 Ⓙ Ⓚ Ⓛ ●

1 Ⓐ ● Ⓒ Ⓓ   3 Ⓐ Ⓑ ● Ⓓ

Lesson 8: Using Correct Expression

Language Skill: Identifying sentences that are the clearest, most correct, and most concise examples of effective writing

SAY: **Turn to Lesson 8, Using Correct Expression, on page 23.**

Check to see that all students find Lesson 8.

SAY: **In Lesson 8 you will practice choosing the sentence or sentences that express an idea most correctly and most clearly.**

Read the Directions to students.

SAY: **Now look at Try This.**

Read Try This to students.

SAY: **Now look at S1. Read the sentences silently. Then darken the circle for the sentence or sentences that express the idea most correctly and most clearly.**

Allow students time to choose and mark their answer.

SAY: **Now look at Think It Through.**

Read Think It Through to students. Check to see that all students have filled in the correct answer space. Ask students if they have any questions.

4   **J**   Before eating, raccoons wash their hands as a habit.

     K   It's a habit for raccoons to wash their hands eating.

     L   Raccoons have a habit of washing their hands before eating.

     M   Washing their hands is a habit before raccoons eating.

5   **A**   The squirrel ran along the top of the roof.

     B   Along the squirrel ran the top of the roof.

     C   On the roof top, along ran the squirrel.

     D   The squirrel along the top of the roof ran.

6   **J**   In her chair fell asleep Lucia.

     K   Lucia asleep. She fell in her chair.

     L   Asleep in her chair fell Lucia.

     M   Lucia fell asleep in her chair.

7   **A**   Under water for two minutes can dolphins stay.

     B   Dolphins can stay under water for two minutes.

     C   Stay under dolphins. Water can for two minutes.

     D   For two minutes can dolphins under water stay.

8   **J**   When Mrs. Hernández folding the clothes, dry they were.

     K   Mrs. Hernández folded the clothes when they were dry.

     L   Dry were they when Mrs. Hernández folded the clothes.

     M   Folding the clothes when they were dry was Mrs. Hernández.

STOP

Answers

     4 ⓙ ⓚ ● Ⓜ   6 ⓙ ⓚ ⓛ ●   8 ⓙ ● ⓛ Ⓜ

24   5 ● Ⓑ Ⓒ Ⓓ   7 Ⓐ ● Ⓒ Ⓓ

Now you will practice choosing more sentences that express an idea most correctly and clearly. Put your finger on number 1. Do numbers 1 through 8 just as we did S1. When you come to the words *GO ON* at the bottom of the page, continue working on the next page. When you come to the word *STOP* at the bottom of page 24, put your pencils down. You may now begin.

Allow students time to choose and mark their answers.

Review the questions and answer choices with students. Discuss with the class why one answer is correct and the others are not correct. Also check to see that students have carefully filled in their answer spaces and have completely erased any stray marks.

Lesson 9: Analyzing Paragraphs

Directions: Darken the circle for the correct answer.

> **TRY THIS** Study each answer choice carefully before choosing your answer. Check yourself by looking back at the paragraph.

S1 [1] Usually we read or play games. [2] Last week my family and I went to the park. [3] We took a picnic and hiked in the woods. [4] We had so much fun that we are going again next week.

Which is the best opening sentence for this paragraph?

A I like to hike.

B My family and I like to spend time together.

C My sister likes to go places.

D We cooked hot dogs on the grill.

> **THINK IT THROUGH** The correct answer is **B**. The sentence for choice B tells what the paragraph is about. Choices A and C are too general. Choice D could be used in the paragraph, but it is not a good first sentence.

STOP

[1] Steve and I go to the movies every month. [2] We always sit in the front row. [3] We like the funny movies the best. [4] My sister likes the cartoons. [5] Sometimes we spill it because we laugh so hard. [6] Steve and I always get popcorn to eat.

1 Which is the best opening sentence for this paragraph?

A Our friends like to join us at the movies.

B Funny movies make us laugh.

C I like funny movies.

D Going to the movies is fun!

2 Where does sentence 5 belong in this paragraph?

J Between sentences 1 and 2

K Before sentence 3

L After sentence 6

M Where it is now

3 Which sentence does not belong in this paragraph?

A Sentence 2   C Sentence 4

B Sentence 3   D Sentence 6

GO ON

Level 9

Answers
S1 Ⓐ ● Ⓒ Ⓓ   2 Ⓙ Ⓚ ● Ⓜ
1 Ⓐ Ⓑ Ⓒ ●   3 Ⓐ Ⓑ ● Ⓓ

25

Lesson 9: Analyzing Paragraphs

Language Skills: Determining the topic and supporting details of a paragraph; determining sentence order in a paragraph

SAY: **Turn to Lesson 9, Analyzing Paragraphs, on page 25.**

Check to see that all students find Lesson 9.

SAY: **In Lesson 9 you will practice answering questions about paragraphs.**

Read the Directions to students.

SAY: **Now look at Try This.**

Read Try This to students.

SAY: **Now look at S1. Read the paragraph silently. Then read the question and the answer choices carefully. Which is the best opening sentence for this paragraph? Darken the circle for the correct answer.**

Allow students time to choose and mark their answer.

SAY: **Now look at Think It Through.**

Read Think It Through to students. Check to see that all students have filled in the correct answer space. Ask students if they have any questions.

¹ But the worst is when I hit the ball over the fence! ² I need lots of practice. ³ Many times I hit the ball right into the net. ⁴ I'm a good roller skater. ⁵ Sometimes I hit the ball into the next court.

4 **Where does sentence 1 belong in this paragraph?**

J   Where it is now

K   After sentence 2

L   Between sentences 4 and 5

M   After sentence 5

5 **Which sentence does _not_ belong in this paragraph?**

A   Sentence 1

B   Sentence 2

C   Sentence 4

D   Sentence 5

6 **Which is the best ending sentence for this paragraph?**

J   Someday I will be the world's best tennis player.

K   I need to practice every day to become a better tennis player.

L   My friends play tennis, too.

M   My teacher is a good tennis player.

¹ Marvin's mother was watering the garden. ² He found a jar of jelly. ³ Marvin looked in the refrigerator to find something to eat. ⁴ But there was no peanut butter to make a peanut butter and jelly sandwich. ⁵ Just then, Marvin's dad walked in with a grocery bag.

7 **Which is the best opening sentence for this paragraph?**

A   Marvin always eats lunch at noon.

B   Peanut butter is made from peanuts.

C   Marvin went to the kitchen to fix lunch.

D   Marvin's dad went grocery shopping.

8 **Which sentence does _not_ belong in this paragraph?**

J   Sentence 1

K   Sentence 2

L   Sentence 3

M   Sentence 5

9 **Where does sentence 2 belong in this paragraph?**

A   After sentence 4

B   After sentence 5

C   Between sentences 3 and 4

D   Where it is now

STOP

Level 9

Answers

26

4 Ⓙ Ⓚ Ⓛ ●   6 Ⓙ ● Ⓛ Ⓜ   8 ● Ⓚ Ⓛ Ⓜ

5 Ⓐ Ⓑ ● Ⓓ   7 Ⓐ Ⓑ ● Ⓓ   9 Ⓐ Ⓑ ● Ⓓ

SAY: **Now you will practice answering more questions about paragraphs. Put your finger on number 1. Do numbers 1 through 9 just as we did S1. When you come to the words _GO ON_ at the bottom of the page, continue working on the next page. When you come to the word _STOP_ at the bottom of page 26, put your pencils down. You may now begin.**

Allow students time to choose and mark their answers.

Review the questions and answer choices with students. Discuss with the class why one answer is correct and the others are not correct. Also check to see that students have carefully filled in their answer spaces and have completely erased any stray marks.

Unit 4 Test

S1   **A**   In August Ling will fly to

     B   Taiwan. she will visit her

     C   grandparents for two weeks.

     D   *(No mistakes)*

STOP

S2   **J**   Pam has a saltwater fish

     K   tank with sea horses in it.

     L   Would you like to see it

     M   *(No mistakes)*

STOP

S3   **A**   Tim couldn't get into

     B   his house because he

     C   forgetted his key.

     D   *(No mistakes)*

STOP

For questions 1–7, darken the circle for the line that has a capitalization error. Darken the circle for *No mistakes* if there is no error.

1   **A**   The city swimming pool

     B   on Beaver Lane closes

     C   in september for the winter.

     D   *(No mistakes)*

2   **J**   We wear red, white, and blue

     K   clothes and wave the American

     L   flag on the fourth of july.

     M   *(No mistakes)*

3   **A**   We need to go to the library

     B   to find some Information

     C   about Queen Elizabeth.

     D   *(No mistakes)*

4   **J**   When I got home from school,

     K   I saw mr. Crew walking his

     L   dog through the neighborhood.

     M   *(No mistakes)*

5   **A**   My mother always reminds

     B   me to wash my hands with

     C   soap and hot water before i eat.

     D   *(No mistakes)*

6   **J**   Harry ordered a pizza but

     K   forgot to tell the driver to

     L   deliver it to 301 circle drive.

     M   *(No mistakes)*

7   **A**   We have a pet lizard named

     B   Herman. We found him when

     C   we went to the colorado river.

     D   *(No mistakes)*

GO ON

Level 9

Answers

S1 Ⓐ ● Ⓒ Ⓓ   S3 Ⓐ Ⓑ ● Ⓓ   2 Ⓙ Ⓚ ● Ⓜ   4 Ⓙ ● Ⓛ Ⓜ   6 Ⓙ Ⓚ ● Ⓜ

S2 Ⓙ Ⓚ ● Ⓜ   1 Ⓐ Ⓑ ● Ⓓ   3 ● Ⓑ Ⓒ Ⓓ   5 Ⓐ Ⓑ ● Ⓓ   7 Ⓐ Ⓑ ● Ⓓ   **27**

Unit 4 Test

SAY: **Turn to the Unit 4 Test on page 27.**

Check to see that all students find the Unit 4 Test.

SAY: **In this test you will use the language skills that we have practiced in this unit. Look at S1. Read the sentences. Then darken the circle for the line that has an error in capitalization. Darken the circle for *No mistakes* if there is no error.**

Allow students time to choose and mark their answer.

SAY: **You should have darkened the circle for choice *B*. The word *she* should be capitalized because it is the first word of the second sentence.**

Check to see that all students have filled in the correct answer space. Ask students if they have any questions.

SAY: **Now look at S2. Read the sentences. Then darken the circle for the line that has an error in punctuation. Darken the circle for *No mistakes* if there is no error.**

Allow students time to choose and mark their answer.

SAY: **You should have darkened the circle for choice *L*. The second sentence should end with a question mark because it asks a question.**

Check to see that all students have filled in the correct answer space. Ask students if they have any questions.

SAY: **Now look at S3. Read the sentence. Then darken the circle for the line that has an error in the way the words are used. If there is no error, darken the circle for *No mistakes*.**

Allow students time to choose and mark their answer.

SAY: **You should have darkened the circle for choice *C*. The word *forgetted* is an error. *Forgot* is the word that should have been used.**

Check to see that all students have filled in the correct answer space. Ask students if they have any questions.

Unit 4 Test

S1
A In August Ling will fly to
B Taiwan. she will visit her
C grandparents for two weeks.
D *(No mistakes)*

— STOP

S2
J Pam has a saltwater fish
K tank with sea horses in it.
L Would you like to see it
M *(No mistakes)*

— STOP

S3
A Tim couldn't get into
B his house because he
C forgetted his key.
D *(No mistakes)*

— STOP

For questions 1–7, darken the circle for the line that has a capitalization error. Darken the circle for *No mistakes* if there is no error.

1
A The city swimming pool
B on Beaver Lane closes
C in september for the winter.
D *(No mistakes)*

2
J We wear red, white, and blue
K clothes and wave the American
L flag on the fourth of july.
M *(No mistakes)*

3
A We need to go to the library
B to find some Information
C about Queen Elizabeth.
D *(No mistakes)*

4
J When I got home from school,
K I saw mr. Crew walking his
L dog through the neighborhood.
M *(No mistakes)*

5
A My mother always reminds
B me to wash my hands with
C soap and hot water before i eat.
D *(No mistakes)*

6
J Harry ordered a pizza but
K forgot to tell the driver to
L deliver it to 301 circle drive.
M *(No mistakes)*

7
A We have a pet lizard named
B Herman. We found him when
C we went to the colorado river.
D *(No mistakes)*

GO·ON

Answers
S1 Ⓐ ● Ⓒ Ⓓ   S3 Ⓐ Ⓑ ● Ⓓ   2 Ⓙ Ⓚ ● Ⓜ   4 Ⓙ ● Ⓛ Ⓜ   6 Ⓙ Ⓚ ● Ⓜ
S2 Ⓙ Ⓚ ● Ⓜ   1 Ⓐ Ⓑ ● Ⓓ   3 Ⓐ ● Ⓒ Ⓓ   5 Ⓐ Ⓑ ● Ⓓ   7 Ⓐ Ⓑ ● Ⓓ

Level 9

27

SAY: **Now you will finish the test on your own. Read the directions carefully. Put your finger on number 1. Do numbers 1 through 27 just as we did the samples. Darken the circle for each correct answer. When you come to the words *GO ON* at the bottom of a page, continue working on the next page. When you come to the word *STOP* at the bottom of page 30, put your pencils down. You may now begin.**

Allow students time to choose and mark their answers.

For questions 8–12, darken the circle for the line that has a punctuation error. Darken the circle for *No mistakes* if there is no error.

8   J   Cal brought three books home

     K   from school. He had homework

     L   in English math and science.

     M   *(No mistakes)*

9   A   Lupe stayed home from school.

     B   Cant we make some soup for

     C   Lupe and take it to her house?

     D   *(No mistakes)*

10   J   1326 Front Street

     K   Augusta, GA 30907

     L   September 6 1995

     M   *(No mistakes)*

11   A Dear Mr Johnson,

     B   I just bought the two

     C joke books you wrote this year.

     D   *(No mistakes)*

12   J I think they are great

     K   Your fan,

     L   Yung Chou

     M   *(No mistakes)*

For questions 13–17, darken the circle for the line that has an error in the way the words are used. Darken the circle for *No mistakes* if there is no error.

13   A   After Susan finishes

     B   her homework, she practices

     C   the piano for two hours.

     D   *(No mistakes)*

14   J   "Willya please tell Ling

     K   to stop banging the pots?

     L   I'm trying to study!"

     M   *(No mistakes)*

15   A   Amanda went to the library.

     B   Her borrowed some books

     C   about making birdhouses.

     D   *(No mistakes)*

16   J   Cassie brought her pet

     K   mouses to school for

     L   show and tell.

     M   *(No mistakes)*

17   A   I and my dad look very

     B   much alike. We both have

     C   green eyes and red hair.

     D   *(No mistakes)*

GO ON

For questions 18–20, darken the circle for the word or words that will correct the underlined part of the sentence. Darken the circle for *No change* if there is no error.

18 Ed has missed his parents **although** the minute they left.

J because   K since   L unless   M *(No change)*

19 Next week chicks **have hatched** from those eggs.

A will hatch   B had hatched   C were hatching D *(No change)*

20 Would you rather play catch or swim **in** the pool?

J under   K over   L against   M *(No change)*

For questions 21–23, darken the circle for the line that expresses the idea most clearly.

21 A When she went to the park, the birds Mary fed.

B Mary went to the park when she fed the birds.

C When she fed the birds, Mary went to the park.

D Mary fed the birds when she went to the park.

22 J The book *Swimmy* Leo Lionni wrote.

K *Swimmy* the book, Leo Lionni wrote.

L Leo Lionni wrote the book S*wimmy*.

M Wrote S*wimmy* the book. Leo Lionni.

23 A The circus trainers. The animals eat at five o'clock.

B The trainers at the circus feed the animals at five o'clock.

C The trainers feed the animals at the five o'clock circus.

D The animals at the circus, the trainers feed at five o'clock.

GO ON

Level 9

For questions 24–27, darken the circle for the correct answer.

> [1] Spiders use silk to spin webs. [2] Spiders also use their silk to make sacs to hold their eggs. [3] Many spiders spin a single line of silk wherever they go. [4] They use this "lifeline" to escape from enemies. [5] Some spiders are poisonous. [6] These webs are used for catching prey.

24 Where does sentence 6 belong in this paragraph?

    J Between sentences 1 and 2

    K Between sentences 3 and 4

    L Before sentence 5

    M Where it is now

25 Which is the best ending sentence for this paragraph?

    A Spiders are dangerous.

    B Spiders need the silk thread for safety.

    C Spiders use their silk in many ways.

    D Spiders lay eggs in sacs.

> [1] Last year we invited relatives and friends to our house for Thanksgiving dinner. [2] The children usually behave very well. [3] Three weeks before, we planned a complete menu, from soup to dessert. [4] As soon as we got home, we started cooking and baking. [5] Five days before Thanksgiving, we went shopping for the food. [6] The night before Thanksgiving Day, we set the table.

26 Which is the best opening sentence for this paragraph?

    J We invited fifteen guests for Thanksgiving this year.

    K My mom and I made Thanksgiving dinner all by ourselves.

    L Having a Thanksgiving dinner takes a lot of work and planning.

    M What is the easiest part of a Thanksgiving celebration?

27 Which sentence does not belong in this paragraph?

    A Sentence 2

    B Sentence 3

    C Sentence 4

    D Sentence 5

SAY: **It is now time to stop. You have completed the Unit 4 Test. Make sure you have carefully filled in your answer spaces and have completely erased any stray marks. Then put your pencils down.**

After the test has been scored, review the questions and answer choices with students. If students are having difficulty, provide them with additional practice.

STOP

Level 9

Answers

24 ● Ⓚ Ⓛ Ⓜ   **26** Ⓙ Ⓚ ● Ⓜ

30 **25** Ⓐ Ⓑ ● Ⓓ   **27** ● Ⓑ Ⓒ Ⓓ

UNIT 5 Math Concepts and Estimation

Lesson 10: Working with Numeration

Directions: Darken the circle for the correct answer.

> **TRY THIS**
>
> Read the problem twice before making your answer choice. Be sure to think about which numbers stand for hundreds, tens, and ones.

S1 Which is another name for 9 tens and 3 ones?

A 9031   C 93

B 931   D 903

> **THINK IT THROUGH**
>
> The correct answer is C. There are 9 tens and 3 ones. The 9 should be in the tens place and the 3 should be in the ones place.

STOP

1 Which of the following numbers is greater than 47?

A 18

B 23

C 39

D 53

2 Which number is closest in value to 400?

J 40   L 406

K 392   M 499

3 Which is another way to write 238?

A 20 + 380

B 200 + 30 + 8

C 200 + 30 + 80

D 2000 + 30 + 8

4 Which of the following is another name for 968?

J Ninety six eight

K Nine hundred sixty-eight

L Nine thousand sixty-eight

M Ninety hundred sixty-eight

5 Which of the following numbers should go in the box?

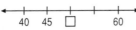

40   45   □   60

A 46

B 50

C 55

D 58

GO ON

Answers

S1 Ⓐ Ⓑ ● Ⓓ   2 Ⓙ Ⓚ ● Ⓜ   4 Ⓙ ● Ⓛ Ⓜ

1 Ⓐ Ⓑ Ⓒ ●   3 Ⓐ ● Ⓒ Ⓓ   5 Ⓐ ● Ⓒ Ⓓ

Level 9

31

UNIT 5 Math Concepts and Estimation

Lesson 10: Working with Numeration

Mathematics Skills: Understanding relative values of numbers; recognizing different names for numbers; understanding place value and expanded notation; comparing and ordering numbers; recognizing odd and even numbers; understanding relative values of currency; identifying fractional parts of sets

SAY: **Turn to Lesson 10, Working with Numeration, on page 31.**

Check to see that all students find Lesson 10.

Distribute scratch paper to students. Tell them that they may use the scratch paper to work the problems.

SAY: **In Lesson 10 you will practice solving problems about numbers.**

Read the Directions to students.

SAY: **Now look at Try This.**

Read Try This to students.

SAY: **Now look at S1. You are asked to choose another name for 9 tens and 3 ones. Look at the answer choices carefully. Then darken the circle for the correct answer.**

Allow students time to choose and mark their answer.

SAY: **Now look at Think It Through.**

Read Think It Through to students. Check to see that all students have filled in the correct answer space. Ask students if they have any questions.

6 Which of these sets is a group of even numbers?

   J 2, 14, 21

   K 3, 13, 18

   L 6, 10, 16

   M 4, 5, 12

7 Which of these sets of coins has the greatest value?

   A 1 quarter

   B 23 pennies

   C 2 dimes

   D 3 nickels

8 Which of the following is another name for 586?

   J Fifty eight six

   K Five thousand eighty-six

   L Five hundred eighty-six

   M Fifty hundred eighty-six

9 Which is the correct way to write 300 + 50 + 2 as one numeral?

   A 352

   B 1000

   C 3052

   D 300,502

10 What fraction of the group of squares are shaded?

   J $\frac{1}{2}$

   K $\frac{1}{3}$

   L $\frac{2}{3}$

   M $\frac{3}{1}$

11 Which of the following numbers is less than 84?

   A 78

   B 85

   C 89

   D 92

12 Which of the following numbers should go in the box?

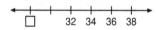

   J 26

   K 28

   L 30

   M 31

STOP

Level 9

Answers

6 Ⓙ Ⓚ ● Ⓜ   **8** Ⓙ Ⓚ ● Ⓜ   **10** Ⓙ Ⓚ ● Ⓜ   **12** Ⓙ ● Ⓛ Ⓜ

32   **7** ● Ⓑ Ⓒ Ⓓ   **9** ● Ⓑ Ⓒ Ⓓ   **11** ● Ⓑ Ⓒ Ⓓ

SAY: **Now you will practice solving more problems about numbers. Put your finger on number 1. Do numbers 1 through 12 just as we did S1. When you come to the words *GO ON* at the bottom of the page, continue working on the next page. When you come to the word *STOP* at the bottom of page 32, put your pencils down. You may now begin.**

Allow students time to choose and mark their answers.

Review the questions and answer choices with students. Discuss with the class why one answer is correct and the others are not correct. Also check to see that students have carefully filled in their answer spaces and have completely erased any stray marks.

Directions: Darken the circle for the correct answer.

| TRY THIS | Work each problem on scratch paper. Try each answer choice in the problem before you choose your answer. |

S1 Which sign should go in the ○ in this number sentence?

| 4 ○ 6 = 24 |

A +   C ×

B −   D ÷

| THINK IT THROUGH | The correct answer is C. If you try each of the symbols in the number sentence, you will find that the only symbol that works is the multiplication sign, because 4 x 6 = 24. |

STOP

1 Pam has 16 seashells in her collection. Her sister Sarah has 11. They have one brother. **Which of these number sentences shows how many more seashells Pam has than Sarah?**

A 16 + 11 = 27

B 16 + 11 + 1 = 28

C 11 − 1 = 10

D 16 − 11 = 5

2 What numeral should go in the □ to make this number sentence correct?

| 4 + 3 + 6 = 3 + □ + 4 |

J 0

K 3

L 4

M 6

3 What is the missing factor in this number sentence?

| □ x 5 = 15 |

A 3

B 10

C 45

D 75

4 What numeral should go in the □ to make this number sentence correct?

| 2 + 5 + 7 = □ + 7 + 2 |

J 1

K 2

L 5

M 7

STOP

Answers

S1 Ⓐ Ⓑ ● Ⓓ   2 Ⓙ Ⓚ Ⓛ ●   4 Ⓙ Ⓚ ● Ⓜ

1 Ⓐ Ⓑ Ⓒ ●   3 ● Ⓑ Ⓒ Ⓓ

Level 9

33

Lesson 11: Working with Number Sentences

Mathematics Skills: Understanding symbols for operations and relationships; recognizing number sentences used to represent problems; solving number sentences; understanding number sentences used to represent number properties

SAY: **Turn to Lesson 11, Working with Number Sentences, on page 33.**

Check to see that all students find Lesson 11.

Distribute scratch paper to students. Tell them that they may use the scratch paper to work the problems.

SAY: **In Lesson 11 you will practice solving problems about number sentences.**

Read the Directions to students.

SAY: **Now look at Try This.**

Read Try This to students.

SAY: **Now look at S1. You are asked to choose the sign that should go in the circle. Look at the answer choices carefully. Then darken the circle for the correct answer.**

Allow students time to choose and mark their answer.

SAY: **Now look at Think It Through.**

Read Think It Through to students. Check to see that all students have filled in the correct answer space. Ask students if they have any questions.

SAY: **Now you will practice solving more problems about number sentences. Put your finger on number 1. Do numbers 1 through 4 just as we did S1. When you come to the word *STOP* at the bottom of the page, put your pencils down. You may now begin.**

Allow students time to choose and mark their answers.

Review the questions and answer choices with students. Discuss with the class why one answer is correct and the others are not correct. Also check to see that students have carefully filled in their answer spaces and have completely erased any stray marks.

Directions: Darken the circle for the correct answer.

 TRY THIS | If a picture is given, study it carefully. If a picture is not given, draw one on your scratch paper to help you check your answer.

S1 What is the area of this shape in square units?

 = 1 square unit

A 2 square units

B 3 square units

C 6 square units

D 8 square units

 THINK IT THROUGH | The correct answer is D, 8 square units. To find the area of the shape, you should count each square. The shape has 8 squares, so the correct answer is 8 square units.

STOP

1 Which figure is made of all triangles?

A

C

B

D

2 Which unit is the best to use to measure the weight of a dog?

J Kilometers

K Pounds

L Inches

M Grams

3 Which of the following shapes is an oval?

A

C

B

D

4 Which of these pictures shows a star outside a closed figure?

J

L

K

M

GO ON

Level 9

34

Answers

S1 Ⓐ Ⓑ Ⓒ ●   2 Ⓙ ● Ⓛ Ⓜ   4 Ⓙ ● Ⓛ Ⓜ

1 Ⓐ Ⓑ Ⓒ ●   3 ● Ⓑ Ⓒ Ⓓ

Lesson 12: Using Measurement and Geometry

Mathematics Skills: Identifying appropriate units of measurement; measuring quantity, time, length, and weight; estimating measurements; recognizing and comparing geometric figures; determining perimeter and area of plane figures; understanding spatial and geometric relationships

SAY: **Turn to Lesson 12, Using Measurement and Geometry, on page 34.**

Check to see that all students find Lesson 12.

Distribute scratch paper to students. Tell them that they may use the scratch paper to work the problems.

SAY: **In Lesson 12 you will practice solving problems about measurement and shapes.**

Read the Directions to students.

SAY: **Now look at Try This.**

Read Try This to students.

SAY: **Now look at S1. You are asked to find the area of the shape in square units. Look at the answer choices carefully. Then darken the circle for the correct answer.**

Allow students time to choose and mark their answer.

SAY: **Now look at Think It Through.**

Read Think It Through to students. Check to see that all students have filled in the correct answer space. Ask students if they have any questions.

5 A family rents a cabin for 1 week each summer. The family arrived on July 21. **On what date did the family leave the cabin?**

A July 14

B July 22

C July 28

D July 31

6 What shape was cut from the piece of folded paper shown here?

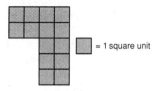

J

K

L

M

7 Which of these has a length that is best measured in feet?

A A book

B A nail

C A hamster

D A bicycle

8 What is the area of this shape in square units?

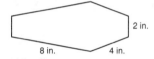

= 1 square unit

J 2 square units

K 4 square units

L 9 square units

M 14 square units

9 What is the perimeter of this figure?

2 in.

8 in. 4 in.

A 24 inches

B 26 inches

C 28 inches

D 30 inches

10 Which of these has a weight that is best measured in grams?

J A cookie

K A bag of potatoes

L A refrigerator

M A car

STOP

Answers

5 Ⓐ Ⓑ ● Ⓓ   7 Ⓐ Ⓑ Ⓒ ●   9 Ⓐ Ⓑ ● Ⓓ

6 ● Ⓚ Ⓛ Ⓜ   8 Ⓙ Ⓚ Ⓛ ●   10 ● Ⓚ Ⓛ Ⓜ

Level 9

35

SAY: **Now you will practice solving more problems about measurement and shapes. Put your finger on number 1. Do numbers 1 through 10 just as we did S1. When you come to the words *GO ON* at the bottom of the page, continue working on the next page. When you come to the word *STOP* at the bottom of page 35, put your pencils down. You may now begin.**

Allow students time to choose and mark their answers.

Review the questions and answer choices with students. Discuss with the class why one answer is correct and the others are not correct. Also check to see that students have carefully filled in their answer spaces and have completely erased any stray marks.

Lesson 13: Using Estimation

Directions: Darken the circle for the correct answer.

TRY THIS	Round the numbers in each problem. Then solve the problem in your head.

S1 Which is the closest estimate of 42 + 59?

A 80

B 90

C 100

D 110

THINK IT THROUGH	The correct answer is C. Since 42 + 59 is about the same as 40 + 60, the closest estimate is 100.

STOP

1 Which is the closest estimate of how many more points the Trailblazers scored than the Mavericks?

Basketball Scores	
Trailblazers	89
Mavericks	53

A 10   C 30

B 20   D 40

2 Which is the closest estimate of how much the plant has grown since September?

September   November

12 inches   38 inches

J 20 inches   L 40 inches

K 30 inches   M 50 inches

3 Which is the closest estimate of the total cost of the clothing?

$3.98 $7.25 $5.09

A $3.00 + $7.00 + $5.00

B $4.00 + $7.00 + $5.00

C $4.00 + $7.00 + $6.00

D $4.00 + $8.00 + $5.00

4 Which is the closest estimate of 644 + 277?

J 700   L 900

K 800   M 1000

GO ON

Level 9

Answers

S1 Ⓐ Ⓑ ● Ⓓ   2 Ⓙ ● Ⓛ Ⓜ   4 Ⓙ Ⓚ ● Ⓜ

1 Ⓐ Ⓑ Ⓒ ●   3 Ⓐ ● Ⓒ Ⓓ

36

Lesson 13: Using Estimation

Mathematics Skills: Rounding; estimating

SAY: **Turn to Lesson 13, Using Estimation, on page 36.**

Check to see that all students find Lesson 13.

SAY: **In Lesson 13 you will practice solving problems about estimation. You will not be allowed to use scratch paper for this lesson, so you must solve the problems in your head.**

Read the <u>Directions</u> to students.

SAY: **Now look at <u>Try This</u>.**

Read <u>Try This</u> to students.

SAY: **Now look at S1. You are asked to choose the closest estimate of 42 + 59. Read the answer choices carefully. Then darken the circle for the correct answer.**

Allow students time to choose and mark their answer.

SAY: **Now look at <u>Think It Through</u>.**

Read <u>Think It Through</u> to students. Check to see that all students have filled in the correct answer space. Ask students if they have any questions.

5 Which is the closest estimate of 4 × 53?

A 2

B 20

C 200

D 2000

6 Which is the closest estimate of the total number of ladybugs?

8 ladybugs   12 ladybugs   19 ladybugs

J 10 + 10 + 10

K 0 + 10 + 20

L 10 + 20 + 20

M 10 + 10 + 20

7 Which is the closest estimate of the total cost of the two toys?

24¢   78¢

A 70¢

B 90¢

C $1.00

D $1.10

8 Which is the closest estimate of 82 + 62?

J Less than 140

K Between 140 and 150

L Between 150 and 160

M More than 170

9 The closest estimate of the total number of apples is _____.

36   42   43   39
apples   apples   apples   apples

A (2 × 30) + (2 × 40)

B (2 × 30) + (2 × 50)

C 4 × 30

D 4 × 40

10 The closest estimate of $959 − $532 is _____.

J $300

K $400

L $500

M $600

STOP

Level 9

Answers

5 Ⓐ Ⓑ ● Ⓓ   7 Ⓐ Ⓑ ● Ⓓ   9 Ⓐ Ⓑ Ⓒ ●

6 Ⓙ Ⓚ Ⓛ ●   8 Ⓙ ● Ⓛ Ⓜ   10 Ⓙ Ⓚ ● Ⓜ

37

Allow students time to choose and mark their answers.

Review the questions and answer choices with students. Discuss with the class why one answer is correct and the others are not correct. Also check to see that students have carefully filled in their answer spaces and have completely erased any stray marks.

S1 Which is the correct way to write 800 + 20 + 5 as one numeral?

A 825

B 1500

C 8025

D 800,205

STOP

For problems 1–18, darken the circle for the correct answer.

1 Which number is closest in value to 500?

A 50

B 491

C 502

D 599

2 Which is another way to write 679?

J 600 + 790

K 600 + 70 + 9

L 600 + 7 + 90

M 60 + 70 + 9

3 Which of these sets of coins has the greatest value?

A 2 quarters

B 4 dimes

C 7 nickels

D 37 pennies

4 What fraction of the group of triangles are shaded?

J $\frac{4}{1}$

K $\frac{1}{4}$

L $\frac{4}{3}$

M $\frac{3}{4}$

5 Which sign should go in the ○ in this number sentence?

$$18 \bigcirc 3 = 6$$

A ÷

B ×

C +

D −

6 What numeral should go in the ☐ to make this number sentence correct?

$$8 + 1 + 9 = 9 + \Box + 1$$

J 0

K 1

L 8

M 9

GO ON

Level 9

Answers

S1 ● Ⓑ Ⓒ Ⓓ   2 Ⓙ ● Ⓛ Ⓜ   4 Ⓙ ● Ⓛ Ⓜ   6 Ⓙ Ⓚ ● Ⓜ

38   1 Ⓐ Ⓑ ● Ⓓ   3 ● Ⓑ Ⓒ Ⓓ   5 ● Ⓑ Ⓒ Ⓓ

Unit 5 Test

Distribute scratch paper to students. Tell them that they may use the scratch paper to work only problems 1–12. They must solve problems 13–18 in their head.

SAY: **Turn to the Unit 5 Test on page 38.**

Check to see that all students find the Unit 5 Test.

SAY: **In this test you will use the mathematics skills that we have practiced in this unit. Look at S1. You are asked to choose the correct way to write 800 + 20 + 5 as one numeral. Read the answer choices carefully. Then darken the circle for the correct answer.**

Allow students time to choose and mark their answer.

SAY: **You should have darkened the circle for choice *A* because *800 + 20 + 5* is written as *825*.**

Check to see that all students have filled in the correct answer space. Ask students if they have any questions.

SAY: **Now you will finish the test on your own. Read the directions carefully. Put your finger on number 1. Do numbers 1 through 18 just as we did S1. Read the problems and the answer choices carefully. Darken the circle for each correct answer. When you come to the words *GO ON* at the bottom of a page, continue working on the next page. When you come to the word *STOP* at the bottom of page 40, put your pencils down. Remember that you may not use scratch paper for numbers 13–18. You may now begin.**

Allow students time to choose and mark their answers.

7 Which sign should go in the ○ in this number sentence?

$$7 \bigcirc 9 = 16$$

A +

B −

C ×

D ÷

8 Eighteen of the students in Maria's class are girls. Twelve are boys. Three parents help with parties. **Which of these number sentences shows how many more girls than boys are in Maria's class?**

J 18 − 12 = 6

K 18 + 12 + 3 = 33

L 12 − 3 = 9

M 18 + 12 = 30

9 Which unit is the best to use to measure the weight of a pencil?

A inches

B tons

C kilograms

D ounces

10 Kyle started a sewing project on May 3. It took 1 week to complete the project. **On what date did Kyle complete the project?**

J April 26

K May 10

L May 11

M June 3

11 What is the area of this shape in square units?

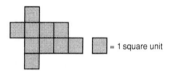
= 1 square unit

A 7 square units

B 8 square units

C 9 square units

D 10 square units

12 Which of these pictures shows a star outside a closed figure?

J   **L**

K   **M**

GO ON

Level 9

13 Which is the closest estimate of the total cost of the calculators?

8 calculators
$2.98 each

A $2.40

B $24.00

C $240

D $2400

14 Which is the closest estimate of $697 – $440?

J $100

K $200

L $300

M $400

15 Which is the closest estimate of the total number of tennis balls?

24 balls   18 balls   28 balls   29 balls

A $(2 \times 20) + (2 \times 30)$

B 4×20

C 4×30

D $(2 \times 40) + (2 \times 30)$

16 Which is the closest estimate of 9×18?

J Between 50 and 100

K Between 100 and 150

L Between 150 and 200

M More than 200

17 The closest estimate of how many more sharks there are than dolphins is _____.

98 sharks   73 dolphins

A 20

B 30

C 40

D 50

18 The closest estimate of how many more tickets were sold on Sunday than on Saturday is _____.

Tickets Sold	
Saturday	119
Sunday	309

J 2

K 20

L 200

M 2000

STOP

Level 9

Answers

13 Ⓐ ● Ⓒ Ⓓ   15 ● Ⓑ Ⓒ Ⓓ   17 Ⓐ ● Ⓒ Ⓓ

14 Ⓙ Ⓚ ● Ⓜ   16 Ⓙ Ⓚ Ⓛ ●   18 Ⓙ Ⓚ ● Ⓜ

40

SAY: **It is now time to stop. You have completed the Unit 5 Test. Make sure you have carefully filled in your answer spaces and have completely erased any stray marks. Then put your pencils down.**

After the test has been scored, review the questions and answer choices with students. If students are having difficulty, provide them with additional practice.

UNIT 6 Math Problems

Lesson 14: Solving Problems

Directions: Darken the circle for the correct answer. Darken the circle for Not given if the answer is not shown.

> **TRY THIS**
>
> Read each problem twice to make sure you understand the question asked. Decide what information is needed and what is not needed. Remember, not all the information given in a word problem may be necessary.

S1 Carl collects models of all kinds. He has 4 model trucks and 5 model cars. He has 2 sisters. **How many models does Carl have altogether?**

A 7

B 9

C 11

D Not given

> **THINK IT THROUGH**
>
> The answer is B. The question asks how many models Carl has. The information "He has two sisters" is not needed to solve the problem. Carl has 4 model trucks and 5 model cars. Since 4 + 5 = 9, Carl has 9 models altogether.

STOP

1 One day at Pine Valley Zoo, 2 baby elephants were born. One weighed 200 pounds. **What else do you need to know to find out how much the baby elephants weighed altogether?**

A The day they were born

B How much the other baby elephant weighed

C How much the baby elephants will weigh when they are adults

D How much each baby elephant's mother weighed

2 The zoo had 50 pounds of bananas. Two zookeepers used 20 pounds of bananas each. **How many pounds of bananas were left?**

J 10   L 90

K 40   M Not given

3 One zookeeper fed 3 black bears and 1 panda bear that was 4 feet tall. Then he fed 4 polar bears and 5 brown bears. **How many bears did he feed?**

A 6   C 15

B 10   D Not given

GO ON

Answers
S1 ⓐ ● ⓒ ⓓ   2 ● Ⓚ Ⓛ Ⓜ
1 ⓐ ● ⓒ ⓓ   3 ⓐ Ⓑ Ⓒ ●

Level 9

41

UNIT 6 Math Problems

Lesson 14: Solving Problems

Mathematics Skills: Solving one-step word problems; solving multiple-step word problems; distinguishing between necessary and extraneous data

SAY: **Turn to Lesson 14, Solving Problems, on page 41.**

Check to see that all students find Lesson 14.

Distribute scratch paper to students. Tell them that they may use the scratch paper to work the problems.

SAY: **In Lesson 14 you will practice solving word problems.**

Read the Directions to students.

SAY: **Now look at Try This.**

Read Try This to students.

SAY: **Now look at S1. Read the problem and the answer choices carefully. Then darken the circle for the correct answer.**

Allow students time to choose and mark their answer.

SAY: **Now look at Think It Through.**

Read Think It Through to students. Check to see that all students have filled in the correct answer space. Ask students if they have any questions.

SAY: **Now you will practice solving more word problems. Put your finger on number 1. Do numbers 1 through 7 just as we did S1. When you come to the words GO ON at the bottom of the page, continue working on the next page. When you come to the word STOP at the bottom of page 42, put your pencils down. You may now begin.**

Allow students time to choose and mark their answers.

This picture shows the school-supply store at Pine Valley Elementary School. Students can use coupons earned in class to buy items from the store. Use the picture to answer questions 4–7.

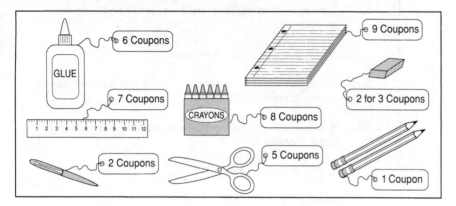

4 Ralph wants to buy a pen, a ruler, and a bottle of glue. **How many coupons does he need?**

J 10

K 15

L 18

M Not given

5 Stephanie bought 2 packages of notebook paper. **How many coupons did she use?**

A 2

B 11

C 18

D Not given

6 Ms. Scott had 45 coupons to give to the science fair winners. She gave each winner the same number of coupons. **What else do you need to know to find out how many coupons she gave each of the winners?**

J How many winners there were

K How she got the coupons

L How many coupons each winner had saved

M How much each item costs

7 Adam bought 6 erasers. **How many coupons did he use?**

A 3

B 6

C 9

D Not given

STOP

Level 9

Lesson 15: Working with Tables and Graphs

Directions: Darken the circle for the correct answer.

> **TRY THIS**
>
> Study each part of the table or graph. Then read each question carefully. Look for words or numbers in the question that tell you what to look for in the table or graph.

S1

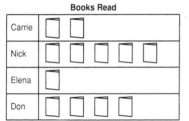

Books Read

Carrie	
Nick	
Elena	
Don	

Who read 5 books?

A Carrie

B Nick

C Elena

D Don

> **THINK IT THROUGH**
>
> The answer is B. Nick read 5 books. First you should find the row that has 5 books. Then look at the beginning of that row to find out who read the 5 books.

STOP

Use the table shown here to answer questions 1–3.

Eye Colors of Three Classes of Third Graders

Color	Class A	Class B	Class C
Blue	13	14	9
Brown	7	10	6
Green	2	2	2
Gray	5	8	4

1 Class A has 7 children with

   A blue eyes.   C green eyes.

   B brown eyes.   D gray eyes.

2 Each class has the same number of children with

   J blue eyes.   L green eyes.

   K brown eyes.   M gray eyes.

3 Class C has twice as many children with gray eyes as

   A blue eyes.

   B brown eyes.

   C green eyes.

   D gray eyes.

GO ON

Level 9

Answers

S1 Ⓐ ● Ⓒ Ⓓ   2 Ⓙ Ⓚ ● Ⓜ

1 Ⓐ ● Ⓒ Ⓓ   3 Ⓐ Ⓑ ● Ⓓ

43

Lesson 15: Working with Tables and Graphs

Mathematics Skills: Interpreting tables and graphs; using data in graphic displays to solve problems

SAY: **Turn to Lesson 15, Working with Tables and Graphs, on page 43.**

Check to see that all students find Lesson 15.

Distribute scratch paper to students. Tell them that they may use the scratch paper to work the problems.

SAY: **In Lesson 15 you will practice using tables and graphs to solve problems.**

Read the <u>Directions</u> to students.

SAY: **Now look at <u>Try This</u>.**

Read <u>Try This</u> to students.

SAY: **Now look at S1. This graph shows the number of books read by 4 students. Study the graph to see what it tells you. Then answer the question. Who read 5 books? Darken the circle for the correct answer.**

Allow students time to choose and mark their answer.

SAY: **Now look at <u>Think It Through</u>.**

Read <u>Think It Through</u> to students. Check to see that all students have filled in the correct answer space. Ask students if they have any questions.

SAY: **Now you will practice using more tables and graphs to solve problems. Put your finger on number 1. Do numbers 1 through 8 just as we did S1. When you come to the words *GO ON* at the bottom of the page, continue working on the next page. When you come to the word *STOP* at the bottom of page 44, put your pencils down. You may now begin.**

Allow students time to choose and mark their answers.

Use the graph shown here to answer questions 4–8.

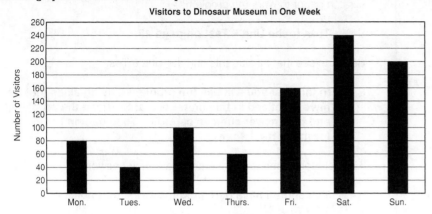

Visitors to Dinosaur Museum in One Week

4 How many days had fewer visitors than Thursday?

J 0   L 2

K 1   M 5

5 How many more people visited the museum on Monday than on Tuesday?

A 10   C 40

B 20   D 60

6 How many people visited the museum on Sunday?

J 180   L 220

K 200   M 240

7 The greatest number of people visited the museum on

A Wednesday   C Saturday

B Friday   D Sunday

8 What can be concluded from this graph?

J The same number of people will visit the museum on Tuesdays and Thursdays.

K There will always be 240 visitors on Saturdays.

L More people will visit the museum on weekends than on weekdays.

M The museum will have about the same number of visitors on a weekday as on the weekends.

STOP

Level 9

Review the questions and answer choices with students. Discuss with the class why one answer is correct and the others are not correct. Also check to see that students have carefully filled in their answer spaces and have completely erased any stray marks.

Answers
4 Ⓙ ● Ⓛ Ⓜ   6 Ⓙ ● Ⓛ Ⓜ   8 Ⓙ Ⓚ ● Ⓜ
5 Ⓐ Ⓑ ● Ⓓ   7 Ⓐ Ⓑ ● Ⓓ

44

S1 Kim taped her favorite songs from the radio. On one tape she recorded 17 songs. On another tape she recorded 15 songs. **How many songs did Kim record?**

A 2

B 25

C 32

D Not given

STOP

For questions 1–15, darken the circle for the correct answer. Darken the circle for Not given if the answer is not shown.

1 Ron and Terri collected insects for their science project. Ron had 8 jars. One day he put 4 insects in each jar. **How many insects did he put in his jars that day?**

A 4   C 32

B 12   D Not given

2 The handle on Terri's butterfly net was 2 feet long. She caught 16 butterflies with her net. The handle on Ron's butterfly net was 3 feet long. He caught 30 butterflies with his net. **To find out how many more butterflies Ron caught than Terri, you should**

J add 30 to 16.

K multiply 2 by 16.

L divide 30 by 3.

M subtract 16 from 30.

3 Ron and Terri found 38 different kinds of moths. They each left 12 at home. They took the rest to school. **How many moths did they take to school?**

A 16

B 24

C 60

D Not given

4 One day Ron caught 4 black beetles and a diving beetle that was 2 inches long. Terri caught 3 bigger diving beetles and 7 tiger beetles. **How many beetles did they catch?**

J 13

K 16

L 17

M Not given

5 The science fair started at 7:00 P.M. **You can find out how long it lasted if you know**

A how many students went.

B how many students won awards.

C what time it ended.

D what time Terri and Ron arrived.

GO ON

Answers
S1 Ⓐ Ⓑ ● Ⓓ   2 Ⓙ Ⓚ Ⓛ ●   4 Ⓙ Ⓚ Ⓛ ●
1 Ⓐ Ⓑ ● Ⓓ   3 Ⓐ Ⓑ Ⓒ ●   5 Ⓐ Ⓑ ● Ⓓ

Level 9

45

Unit 6 Test

Distribute scratch paper to students. Tell them that they may use the scratch paper to work the problems.

SAY: **Turn to the Unit 6 Test on page 45.**

Check to see that all students find the Unit 6 Test.

SAY: **In this test you will use the problem-solving skills that we have practiced in this unit. Look at S1. Read the problem and the answer choices carefully. Then darken the circle for the correct answer.**

Allow students time to choose and mark their answer.

SAY: **You should have darkened the circle for choice _C_ because _17 + 15 = 32._**

Check to see that all students have filled in the correct answer space. Ask students if they have any questions.

SAY: **Now you will finish the test on your own. Read the directions carefully. Put your finger on number 1. Do numbers 1 through 15 just as we did S1. Darken the circle for each correct answer. When you come to the words _GO ON_ at the bottom of a page, continue working on the next page. When you come to the word _STOP_ at the bottom of page 47, put your pencils down. You may now begin.**

Allow students time to choose and mark their answers.

Use the picture shown here to answer questions 6–7.

Sunshine Pet Store

6   Nick bought 3 rabbits. **How much money did he spend?**

     J $5

     K $8

     L $15

     M   Not given

7   Gloria had $22 to spend at the pet store. She bought a snake and a parrot. **What other pet can Gloria buy with the money she has left?**

     A   A turtle

     B   A hamster

     C   A rabbit

     D   None of the pets

Use the table shown here to answer questions 8–9.

How Three Classes of Third Graders Travel to School

Way of Travel	Class 1	Class 2	Class 3
Bus	2	2	2
Bicycle	10	6	6
Walk	8	5	12
Car	7	7	4

8   **How many students in Class 3 ride bicycles to school?**

     J   5   **L**   10

     K   6   **M**   12

9   **How do most students in Class 1 travel to school?**

     A   Car   **C**   Walk

     B   Bus   **D**   Bicycle

GO ON

Level 9

Answers
6 Ⓙ Ⓚ ● Ⓜ   8 Ⓙ ● Ⓛ Ⓜ
7 ● Ⓑ Ⓒ Ⓓ   9 Ⓐ Ⓑ Ⓒ ●

Use the graph shown here to answer questions 10–12.

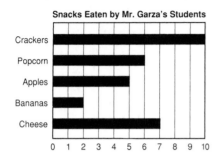

Snacks Eaten by Mr. Garza's Students

10 How many more students eat crackers than cheese?

J 2   L 7

K 3   M 10

11 Which snack is eaten by the fewest number of students?

A Crackers

B Bananas

C Popcorn

D Cheese

12 What kind of snack do exactly five students eat?

J Bananas   L Popcorn

K Apples   M Cheese

Use the graph shown here to answer questions 13–15.

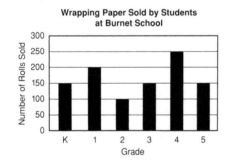

Wrapping Paper Sold by Students at Burnet School

13 How many grades sold fewer rolls of wrapping paper than the first grade?

A 1   C 3

B 2   D 4

14 How many rolls of wrapping paper did the fourth grade sell?

J 150   L 250

K 200   M 300

15 How many more rolls of wrapping paper did the fourth grade sell than kindergarten?

A 50

B 100

C 150

D 200

Answers

10 Ⓙ ● Ⓛ Ⓜ   12 Ⓙ ● Ⓛ Ⓜ   14 Ⓙ Ⓚ ● Ⓜ

11 Ⓐ ● Ⓒ Ⓓ   13 Ⓐ Ⓑ Ⓒ ●   15 Ⓐ ● Ⓒ Ⓓ

STOP

Level 9

47

SAY: **It is now time to stop. You have completed the Unit 6 Test. Make sure you have carefully filled in your answer spaces and have completely erased any stray marks. Then put your pencils down.**

After the test has been scored, review the questions and answer choices with students. If students are having difficulty, provide them with additional practice.

UNIT 7 Math Computation

Lesson 16: Adding

Directions: Darken the circle for the correct answer. Darken the circle for **N** if the answer is not given.

TRY THIS

Add each column of digits. Remember to regroup when necessary. Write the sum and check it against the answer choices.

S1

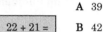
22 + 21 =

A 39
B 42
C 43
D N

THINK IT THROUGH

The correct answer is <u>C</u>. When you add each column of digits, you should get 43.

STOP

1

3 + 6 =

A 6
B 8
C 9
D N

4

42 + 79 =

J 112
K 120
L 121
M N

2

628
+ 464

J 1082
K 1092
L 1192
M N

5

153 + 2 + 34 =

A 188
B 189
C 199
D N

3

286
+ 72

A 258
B 272
C 358
D N

6

67
+ 28

J 41
K 85
L 94
M N

STOP

Level 9

Answers

S1 Ⓐ Ⓑ ● Ⓓ   2 Ⓙ ● Ⓛ Ⓜ   4 Ⓙ Ⓚ ● Ⓜ   6 Ⓙ Ⓚ Ⓛ ●

48   1 Ⓐ Ⓑ ● Ⓓ   3 Ⓐ Ⓑ ● Ⓓ   5 Ⓐ ● Ⓒ Ⓓ

UNIT 7 Math Computation

Lesson 16: Adding

Mathematics Skill: Horizontal and vertical addition of whole numbers

Distribute scratch paper to students. Tell them that they may use the scratch paper to work the problems.

SAY: **Turn to Lesson 16, Adding, on page 48.**

Check to see that all students find Lesson 16.

SAY: **In Lesson 16 you will practice adding numbers.**

Read the Directions to students.

SAY: **Now look at Try This.**

Read Try This to students.

SAY: **Now look at S1. You are asked to add 22 and 21. Work the problem; then darken the circle for the correct answer. Darken the circle for N if the answer is not given.**

Allow students time to choose and mark their answer.

SAY: **Now look at Think It Through.**

Read Think It Through to students. Check to see that all students have filled in the correct answer space. Ask students if they have any questions.

SAY: **Now you will practice solving more addition problems. Put your finger on number 1. Do numbers 1 through 6 just as we did S1. When you come to the word *STOP* at the bottom of the page, put your pencils down. You may now begin.**

Allow students time to choose and mark their answers.

Review the questions and answer choices with students. Discuss with the class why one answer is correct and the others are not correct. Also check to see that students have carefully filled in their answer spaces and have completely erased any stray marks.

Lesson 17: Subtracting

Directions: Darken the circle for the correct answer. Darken the circle for <u>N</u> if the answer is <u>not</u> given.

TRY THIS	Be sure to keep the columns lined up correctly, and remember to regroup when necessary. Check subtraction problems by covering the first number in the problem and adding the second number and your answer. This should equal the first number.

S1

A 15
B 35
C 37
D N

THINK IT THROUGH	The correct answer is <u>A</u>. You can check this by adding the answer to the smaller number. Since 15 + 11 = 26, you know 15 is the correct answer.

STOP

1   74 − 26 =

A 48
B 52
C 100
D N

4   84 − 9 =

J 75
K 76
L 85
M N

2   443 − 21 =

J 322
K 422
L 464
M N

5   854 − 3 =

A 801
B 857
C 871
D N

3   675
    −124

A 541
B 551
C 799
D N

6   774
    − 51

J 723
K 751
L 825
M N

STOP
Level 9

Answers
S1 ● ⒝ ⒞ ⒟   2 ⒥ ● ⒧ ⓜ   4 ● ⓚ ⒧ ⓜ   6 ● ⓚ ⒧ ⓜ
1 ● ⒝ ⒞ ⒟   3 ⒜ ● ⒞ ⒟   5 ⒜ ⒝ ⒞ ●

49

Lesson 17: Subtracting

Mathematics Skill: Horizontal and vertical subtraction of whole numbers

Distribute scratch paper to students. Tell them that they may use the scratch paper to work the problems.

SAY: **Turn to Lesson 17, Subtracting, on page 49.**

Check to see that all students find Lesson 17.

SAY: **In Lesson 17 you will practice subtracting numbers.**

Read the <u>Directions</u> to students.

SAY: **Now look at Try This.**

Read <u>Try This</u> to students.

SAY: **Now look at S1. You are asked to subtract 11 from 26. Work th** **problem; then darken the circle for the correct answer. Darke** **the circle for *N* if the answer is not given.**

Allow students time to choose and mark their answer.

SAY: **Now look at Think It Through.**

Read <u>Think It Through</u> to students. Check to see that all students have filled in the correct answer space. Ask students if they have any question

SAY: **Now you will practice solving more subtraction problems. Put** **your finger on number 1. Do numbers 1 through 6 just as we** **did S1. When you come to the word *STOP* at the bottom of th** **page, put your pencils down. You may now begin.**

Allow students time to choose and mark their answers.

Review the questions and answer choices with students. Discuss with th class why one answer is correct and the others are not correct. Also che to see that students have carefully filled in their answer spaces and have completely erased any stray marks.

Lesson 18: Multiplying

Directions: Darken the circle for the correct answer. Darken the circle for <u>N</u> if the answer is <u>not</u> given.

> **TRY THIS**
>
> Remember, multiplying is like adding over and over again. The second number tells you how many of the first number you should add together.

S1 $13 \times 4 =$

  A 42
  B 47
  C 52
  D N

> **THINK IT THROUGH**
>
> The correct answer is <u>C</u>. Multiplying 13 by 4 is the same as adding four thirteens. Since 13 + 13 + 13 + 13 = 52, you know 13 x 4 is also 52.

STOP

---

1 $8 \times 4 =$

  A 4
  B 12
  C 32
  D N

4
$$\begin{array}{r} 3000 \\ \times\ 4 \\ \hline \end{array}$$

  J 1200
  K 3004
  L 12,000
  M N

2 $602 \times 4 =$

  J 1008
  K 1608
  L 2408
  M N

5
$$\begin{array}{r} 722 \\ \times\ 4 \\ \hline \end{array}$$

  A 726
  B 1122
  C 2888
  D N

3
$$\begin{array}{r} 24 \\ \times\ 3 \\ \hline \end{array}$$

  A 27
  B 62
  C 77
  D N

6 $2 \times 533 =$

  J 535
  K 733
  L 1066
  M N

STOP

Level 9

Answers
S1 Ⓐ Ⓑ ● Ⓓ   2 Ⓙ Ⓚ ● Ⓜ   4 Ⓙ Ⓚ ● Ⓜ   6 Ⓙ Ⓚ ● Ⓜ
1 Ⓐ Ⓑ ● Ⓓ   3 Ⓐ Ⓑ Ⓒ ●   5 Ⓐ Ⓑ ● Ⓓ

50

Lesson 18: Multiplying

Mathematics Skill: Horizontal and vertical multiplication of whole numbers

Distribute scratch paper to students. Tell them that they may use the scratch paper to work the problems.

SAY: **Turn to Lesson 18, Multiplying, on page 50.**

Check to see that all students find Lesson 18.

SAY: **In Lesson 18 you will practice multiplying numbers.**

Read the <u>Directions</u> to students.

SAY: **Now look at <u>Try This</u>.**

Read <u>Try This</u> to students.

SAY: **Now look at S1. You are asked to multiply 13 by 4. Work the problem; then darken the circle for the correct answer. Darken the circle for *N* if the answer is not given.**

Allow students time to choose and mark their answer.

SAY: **Now look at <u>Think It Through</u>.**

Read <u>Think It Through</u> to students. Check to see that all students have filled in the correct answer space. Ask students if they have any questions.

SAY: **Now you will practice solving more multiplication problems. Put your finger on number 1. Do numbers 1 through 6 just as we did S1. When you come to the word *STOP* at the bottom of the page, put your pencils down. You may now begin.**

Allow students time to choose and mark their answers.

Review the questions and answer choices with students. Discuss with the class why one answer is correct and the others are not correct. Also check to see that students have carefully filled in their answer spaces and have completely erased any stray marks.

Lesson 19: Dividing

Directions: Darken the circle for the correct answer. Darken the circle for <u>N</u> if the answer is <u>not</u> given.

| TRY THIS | Check the answer to a division problem by multiplying. Multiply the answer by the divisor (the number you divided by). That answer should equal the number you divided. |

S1

$54 \div 9 =$

- A 6
- B 45
- C 63
- D N

| THINK IT THROUGH | The correct answer is <u>A</u>. You can check this by multiplying 6 by 9. Since 6 x 9 = 54, you know the answer is correct. |

STOP

1 $42 \div 6 =$
- A 7
- B 8
- C 21
- D N

2 $72 \div 9 =$
- J 5
- K 6
- L 8
- M N

3 $48 \div 6 =$
- A 5
- B 6
- C 7
- D N

4 $24 \div 4 =$
- J 4
- K 5
- L 6
- M N

5 $9 \div 3 =$
- A 2
- B 3
- C 6
- D N

6 $64 \div 8 =$
- J 7
- K 8
- L 9
- M N

STOP

Level 9

Answers
S1 ● Ⓑ Ⓒ Ⓓ   2 Ⓙ Ⓚ ● Ⓜ   4 Ⓙ Ⓚ ● Ⓜ   6 Ⓙ ● Ⓛ Ⓜ
1 ● Ⓑ Ⓒ Ⓓ   3 Ⓐ Ⓑ Ⓒ ●   5 Ⓐ ● Ⓒ Ⓓ

51

Lesson 19: Dividing

Mathematics Skill: Division of whole numbers

Distribute scratch paper to students. Tell them that they may use the scratch paper to work the problems.

SAY: **Turn to Lesson 19, Dividing, on page 51.**

Check to see that all students find Lesson 19.

SAY: **In Lesson 19 you will practice dividing numbers.**

Read the Directions to students.

SAY: **Now look at Try This.**

Read Try This to students.

SAY: **Now look at S1. You are asked to divide 54 by 9. Work the problem; then darken the circle for the correct answer. Darken the circle for *N* if the answer is not given.**

Allow students time to choose and mark their answer.

SAY: **Now look at Think It Through.**

Read Think It Through to students. Check to see that all students have filled in the correct answer space. Ask students if they have any questions.

SAY: **Now you will practice solving more division problems. Put your finger on number 1. Do numbers 1 through 6 just as we did S1. When you come to the word *STOP* at the bottom of the page, put your pencils down. You may now begin.**

Allow students time to choose and mark their answers.

Review the questions and answer choices with students. Discuss with the class why one answer is correct and the others are not correct. Also check to see that students have carefully filled in their answer spaces and have completely erased any stray marks.

S1

	A	83
49	B	84
+ 44	C	94
	D	N

STOP

For problems 1–9, darken the circle for the correct answer. Darken the circle for <u>N</u> if the answer is <u>not</u> given.

1

	A	1566
927 + 649 =	B	1576
	C	2676
	D	N

2

	J	5
13 + 8 =	K	15
	L	21
	M	N

3

	A	39
46 – 7 =	B	41
	C	53
	D	N

4

	J	37
85	K	43
– 48	L	47
	M	N

5

	A	131
594 – 63 =	B	531
	C	533
	D	N

6

	J	162
48 × 4 =	K	183
	L	192
	M	N

7

	A	2164
721	B	2864
× 4	C	2884
	D	N

8

	J	6
49 ÷ 7 =	K	7
	L	8
	M	N

9

	A	7
54 ÷ 6 =	B	8
	C	9
	D	N

STOP
Level 9

Answers
S1 ⒶⒷⒸ● 　2 ⓊⓀ●Ⓜ 　4 ●ⓀⓁⓂ 　6 Ⓙ Ⓚ●Ⓜ 　8 Ⓙ●ⓁⓂ
52 　1 Ⓐ●ⒸⒹ 　3 ●ⒷⒸⒹ 　5 Ⓐ●ⒸⒹ 　7 ⒶⒷ●Ⓓ 　9 ⒶⒷ●Ⓓ

Unit 7 Test

Distribute scratch paper to students. Tell them that they may use the scratch paper to work the problems.

SAY: **Turn to the Unit 7 Test on page 52.**

Check to see that all students find the Unit 7 Test.

SAY: **In this test you will use the mathematics skills that we have practiced in this unit. Look at S1. You are asked to add 49 and 44. Darken the circle for the correct answer. Darken the circle for N if the answer is not given.**

Allow students time to choose and mark their answer.

SAY: **You should have darkened the circle for choice D because 49 + 44 = 93, and 93 is not given.**

Ask students if they have any questions.

SAY: **Now you will finish the test on your own. Read the directions carefully. Put your finger on number 1. Do numbers 1 through 9 just as we did the sample. Read the problems and the answer choices carefully. Darken the circle for each correct answer. When you come to the word STOP at the bottom of the page, put your pencils down. You may now begin.**

Allow students time to choose and mark their answers.

SAY: **It is now time to stop. You have completed the Unit 7 Test. Make sure you have carefully filled in your answer spaces and have completely erased any stray marks. Then put your pencils down.**

After the test has been scored, review the questions and answer choices with students. If students are having difficulty, provide them with additional practice.

UNIT 8 Maps and Diagrams

Lesson 20: Working with Maps

Directions: Darken the circle for the correct answer.

> **TRY THIS**
> Study all the information given in the map. Then read each question carefully.

S1

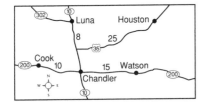

Which city is farthest east?

A Luna

B Watson

C Houston

D Cook

> **THINK IT THROUGH**
> The correct answer is C. According to the compass rose, the map shows that the city that is farthest east is Houston.

STOP

Use the road map in S1 to answer questions 1–4.

1 Which two highways pass through Luna?

A Highway 302 and Highway 10

B Highway 200 and Highway 302

C Highway 10 and Highway 35

D Highway 200 and Highway 35

3 Through how many cities does Highway 200 pass?

A One

B Two

C Three

D Four

2 Which city is directly north of Chandler?

J Luna   L Cook

K Watson   M Houston

4 How many miles is it from Chandler to Watson?

J 20 miles   L 12 miles

K 15 miles   M 10 miles

GO ON

Level 9

Answers
S1 Ⓐ Ⓑ ● Ⓓ   2 ● Ⓚ Ⓛ Ⓜ   4 Ⓙ ● Ⓛ Ⓜ
1 ● Ⓑ Ⓒ Ⓓ   3 Ⓐ Ⓑ ● Ⓓ

53

Study Skills: Using standard map symbols and keys to locate places; determining direction and distance; interpreting and drawing inferences from data

SAY: **Turn to Lesson 20, Working with Maps, on page 53.**

Check to see that all students find Lesson 20.

SAY: **In Lesson 20 you will practice using maps to answer questions**

Read the Directions to students.

SAY: **Now look at Try This.**

Read Try This to students.

SAY: **Now look at S1. Study the road map to see where places are located. Study the compass rose to find directions. Then answer the question. Which city is farthest east? Darken the circle for the correct answer.**

Allow students time to choose and mark their answer.

SAY: **Now look at Think It Through.**

Read Think It Through to students. Check to see that all students have filled in the correct answer space. Ask students if they have any question

Use the map shown here to answer questions 5–10.

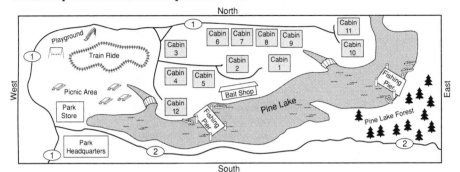

5 Which is closest to cabin 5?

  A The bait shop

  B Pine Lake Forest

  C Cabin 8

  D The playground

6 Carlos walked from cabin 9 to cabin 6.
In which direction did he go?

  J North   **L** East

  K South   **M** West

7 What is between the bait shop and
Pine Lake Forest?

  A The picnic area

  B Park headquarters

  C Pine Lake

  D Highway 2

8 How many fishing piers are shown on
the map?

  J One   **L** Three

  K Two   **M** Four

9 Where is the park headquarters?

  A North of the park store

  B Next to the fishing pier

  C On the south side of the park

  D On the east side of the park

10 Which would be the shortest way
to travel between cabin 1 and
Pine Lake Forest?

  J By boat across Pine Lake

  K By train through the forest

  L By taking Highway 1

  M By taking Highway 2

STOP

Level 9

Answers
5 ● Ⓑ Ⓒ Ⓓ   7 Ⓐ Ⓑ ● Ⓓ   9 Ⓐ Ⓑ ● Ⓓ

54   6 Ⓙ Ⓚ Ⓛ ●   8 Ⓙ ● Ⓛ Ⓜ   10 ● Ⓚ Ⓛ Ⓜ

SAY: **Now you will practice answering more questions about maps. Put your finger on number 1. Do numbers 1 through 10 just as we did S1. When you come to the words *GO ON* at the bottom of the page, continue working on the next page. When you come to the word *STOP* at the bottom of page 54, put your pencils down. You may now begin.**

Allow students time to choose and mark their answers.

Review the questions and answer choices with students. Discuss with the class why one answer is correct and the others are not correct. Also check to see that students have carefully filled in their answer spaces and have completely erased any stray marks.

Lesson 21: Working with Charts and Diagrams

Directions: Darken the circle for the correct answer.

TRY THIS | Study the chart or diagram carefully. Look for key words or numbers in the question that tell you what to look for in the chart or diagram.

S1

Name	Mon.	Tues.	Wed.	Thurs.	Fri.	Sat.
Lupe	⚾	⚾		⚾		
Andrés	✎		🛼	✎		🛼

Basketball ⚾
Art ✎
Roller-skating 🛼

What class does Andrés have after school on Wednesday?

A Basketball

B Art

C Roller-skating

D Football

THINK IT THROUGH | The correct answer is C. To find the answer, look for Andrés's name on the left side of the chart. Then find Wednesday at the top. Put your finger on the place where the two meet. The picture of a roller skate tells you this is the class Andrés has on Wednesday.

STOP

Use the calendar shown here to answer questions 1–3.

FEBRUARY						
Sun.	Mon.	Tues.	Wed.	Thurs.	Fri.	Sat.
		1	2	3	4	5
6	7	8	9	10	11	12
13	14	15	16	17	18	19
20	21	22	23	24	25	26
27	28					

1   Valentine's Day is on February 14th. **What day is that?**

A Monday   C Wednesday

B Tuesday   D Thursday

2   How many Saturdays are there in **February?**

J Three   L Five

K Four   M Six

3   Palak's math project was due on February 1st. He turned it in on February 4th. **How many days late was Palak's project?**

A Two   C Four

B Three   D Five

GO ON

Answers
S1 Ⓐ Ⓑ ● Ⓓ   2 Ⓙ ● Ⓛ Ⓜ
1 ● Ⓑ Ⓒ Ⓓ   3 Ⓐ ● Ⓒ Ⓓ

Level 9

55

Lesson 21: Working with Charts and Diagrams

Study Skills: Using charts and diagrams to find information; determining relationships; making inferences; comparing amounts

SAY: **Turn to Lesson 21, Working with Charts and Diagrams, on page 55.**

Check to see that all students find Lesson 21.

SAY: **In Lesson 21 you will practice using charts and diagrams to answer questions.**

Read the Directions to students.

SAY: **Now look at Try This.**

Read Try This to students.

SAY: **Now look at S1. This diagram shows the kinds of classes Lupe and Andrés take after school. Study the diagram to see what it tells you. Then answer the question. What class does Andrés have after school on Wednesday? Darken the circle for the correct answer.**

Allow students time to choose and mark their answer.

SAY: **Now look at Think It Through.**

Read Think It Through to students. Check to see that all students have filled in the correct answer space. Ask students if they have any questions.

The diagram shown here shows the development of a butterfly. Use the diagram to answer questions 4–5.

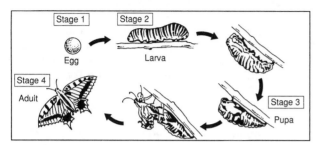

4 What happens in stage 2?

J The pupa becomes an adult butterfly.

K The adult butterfly lays an egg.

L The larva comes out of the egg.

M The larva becomes a pupa.

5 Where would an adult butterfly most likely lay an egg?

A In the ocean

B Under the ground

C Inside a computer

D On a plant

Use the diagram shown here to answer questions 6–7.

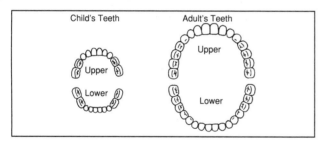

6 Who has 10 lower teeth?

J Adult

K Neither adult nor child

L Child

M Both adult and child

7 How many more upper teeth does an adult have than a child?

A 5   **C** 8

B 6   **D** 12

STOP

Level 9

Answers

4 Ⓙ Ⓚ ● Ⓜ   6 Ⓙ Ⓚ ● Ⓜ

5 Ⓐ Ⓑ Ⓒ ●   7 Ⓐ ● Ⓒ Ⓓ

56

Allow students time to choose and mark their answers.

Review the questions and answer choices with students. Discuss with the class why one answer is correct and the others are not correct. Also check to see that students have carefully filled in their answer spaces and have completely erased any stray marks.

Unit 8 Test

Unit 8 Test

S1

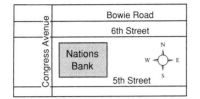

Bowie Road
6th Street

Congress Avenue

Nations Bank

N
W   E
S

5th Street

Which street runs north and south?

A   5th Street

B   6th Street

C   Bowie Road

D   Congress Avenue

STOP

For questions 1–13, darken the circle for the correct answer.

Use this map of a nature park to answer questions 1–4.

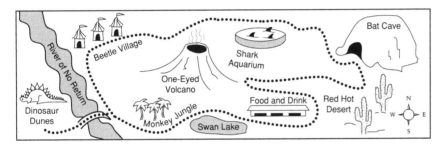

1   **What is between Dinosaur Dunes and Monkey Jungle?**

   A   Beetle Village

   B   One-Eyed Volcano

   C   River of No Return

   D   Red Hot Desert

2   **Where is Beetle Village?**

   J   In the middle of the park

   K   West of the Shark Aquarium

   L   South of Red Hot Desert

   M   East of Swan Lake

3   **How many bridges cross the River of No Return?**

   A   One   C   Three

   B   Two   D   Four

4   **What is directly north of Red Hot Desert?**

   J   Swan Lake

   K   Shark Aquarium

   L   One-Eyed Volcano

   M   Bat Cave

GO ON

Level 9

Answers

S1 Ⓐ Ⓑ Ⓒ ●   2 Ⓙ ● Ⓛ Ⓜ   4 Ⓙ Ⓚ Ⓛ ●

1 Ⓐ Ⓑ ● Ⓓ   3 ● Ⓑ Ⓒ Ⓓ

57

SAY: **Turn to the Unit 8 Test on page 57.**

Check to see that all students find the Unit 8 Test.

SAY: **In this test you will use the map and diagram skills that we have practiced in this unit. Look at S1. Study the street map carefully. Then answer the question. Which street runs north and south? Darken the circle for the correct answer.**

Allow students time to choose and mark their answer.

SAY: **You should have darkened the circle for choice D. Congress Avenue is the only street that runs north and south on this map.**

Check to see that all students have filled in the correct answer space. Ask students if they have any questions.

SAY: **Now you will finish the test on your own. Read the directions carefully. Put your finger on number 1. Do numbers 1 through 13 just as we did S1. Darken the circle for each correct answer. When you come to the words *GO ON* at the bottom of a page, continue working on the next page. When you come to the word *STOP* at the bottom of page 59, put your pencils down. You may now begin.**

Allow students time to choose and mark their answers.

Use the map shown here to answer questions 5–6.

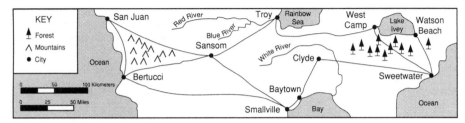

5 On which trip would you travel through a forest?

   A Clyde to Sweetwater

   B West Camp to Sweetwater

   C San Juan to Bertucci

   D Sansom to Troy

6 Which city is most likely to have a paper factory?

   J Baytown

   K Smallville

   L Sansom

   M West Camp

Use the calendar shown here to answer questions 7–9.

OCTOBER

Sun.	Mon.	Tues.	Wed.	Thurs.	Fri.	Sat.
						1
2	3	4	5	6	7	8
9	10	11	12	13	14	15
16	17	18	19	20	21	22
23	24	25	26	27	28	29
30	31					

7 Mr. Tran has a Spanish class every Monday and Tuesday. **How many classes will he have in October?**

   A Seven   **C** Nine

   B Eight   **D** Ten

8 Yuri had to sign up for the race by October 21st. He signed up on October 24th. **How many days late was he?**

   J One   **L** Three

   K Two   **M** Four

9 Mr. Tran's garden club meets on the second Saturday of every month. **What date in October is that?**

   A October 1st

   B October 8th

   C October 15th

   D October 22nd

GO ON

Answers

5 Ⓐ ● Ⓒ Ⓓ   7 Ⓐ Ⓑ ● Ⓓ   9 Ⓐ ● Ⓒ Ⓓ

   6 Ⓙ Ⓚ Ⓛ ●   8 Ⓙ Ⓚ ● Ⓜ

The following diagram shows what happens to cotton plants after they are grown. Use the diagram to answer questions 10–13.

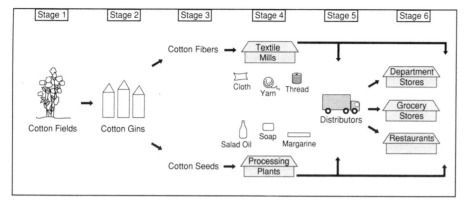

10 Where is the cotton fiber made into cloth?

   J At the cotton fields

   K At the cotton gin

   L At a processing plant

   M At a textile mill

11 What does the cotton gin do?

   A Separates the cotton fiber from the seeds

   B Takes cotton plants to restaurants

   C Plants cotton fields

   D Sells cotton plants to distributors

12 What happens to cotton products in stage 5?

   J They are sent to the cotton gin.

   K They are picked up by distributors.

   L They are made into cotton products.

   M They are delivered to homes.

13 Where does a grocery store most likely get salad oil?

   A From a textile mill

   B From the cotton gins

   C From a distributor

   D From a cotton grower

STOP

After the test has been scored, review the questions and answer choices with students. If students are having difficulty, provide them with additional practice.

Answers

10 Ⓙ Ⓚ Ⓛ ●   12 Ⓙ ● Ⓛ Ⓜ

11 ● Ⓑ Ⓒ Ⓓ   13 Ⓐ Ⓑ ● Ⓓ

Level 9

59

UNIT 9 Reference Materials

Lesson 22: Alphabetizing

Directions: Darken the circle for the word or name that would come <u>first</u> if the words in each group were put in alphabetical order.

TRY THIS	If two or more words in a list have the same first letter, compare the next letters that are different.

S1 A choose

B doctor

C admire

D ballot

THINK IT THROUGH	The correct answer is <u>C</u>. The letter <u>a</u> in <u>admire</u> comes before <u>b</u>, <u>c</u>, and <u>d</u>.

STOP

1 A rave
B snarl
C persuade
D quarry

4 J longhand
K longing
L longhorn
M longitude

2 J Juarez, Abigail
K Steen, Charles
L Messier, Carolyn
M Tran, Matthew

5 A Carillo, Paloma
B Dakkar, Fittnat
C Bauer, Julie
D Emfinger, Billy

3 A McComb, Ashley
B McGhee, Michael
C McRae, Andy
D McDaniels, Issa

6 J busy
K butler
L butcher
M buzzard

STOP

Answers
Level 9

S1 Ⓐ Ⓑ ● Ⓓ   2 ● Ⓚ Ⓛ Ⓜ   4 ● Ⓚ Ⓛ Ⓜ   6 ● Ⓚ Ⓛ Ⓜ
1 Ⓐ Ⓑ ● Ⓓ   3 ● Ⓑ Ⓒ Ⓓ   5 Ⓐ Ⓑ ● Ⓓ

60

UNIT 9 Reference Materials

Lesson 22: Alphabetizing

Study Skill: Alphabetizing words

SAY: **Turn to Lesson 22, Alphabetizing, on page 60.**

Check to see that all students find Lesson 22.

SAY: **In Lesson 22 you will practice alphabetizing words.**

Read the <u>Directions</u> to students.

SAY: **Now look at Try This.**

Read <u>Try This</u> to students.

SAY: **Now look at S1. Study the four answer choices. Which word would come first if these words were put in alphabetical order? Darken the circle for the correct answer.**

Allow students time to choose and mark their answer.

SAY: **Now look at Think It Through.**

Read <u>Think It Through</u> to students. Check to see that all students have filled in the correct answer space. Ask students if they have any questions.

SAY: **Now you will practice alphabetizing more words. Put your finger on number 1. Do numbers 1 through 6 just as we did S1. When you come to the word *STOP* at the bottom of the page, put your pencils down. You may now begin.**

Allow students time to choose and mark their answers.

Review the questions and answer choices with students. Discuss with the class why one answer is correct and the others are not correct. Also check to see that students have carefully filled in their answer spaces and have completely erased any stray marks.

Lesson 23: Using a Table of Contents

Directions: Darken the circle for the correct answer.

TRY THIS Study the table of contents carefully. Be sure that you understand what kind of information can be found in each chapter.

S1 On what page does Chapter 2 begin?

A Page 1

B Page 29

C Page 55

D Page 62

THINK IT THROUGH The correct answer is B. Chapter 2 begins on page 29. The third column of the table of contents lists the page number on which each chapter begins.

STOP

Weather on Our Earth

Contents

1 Which chapter would most likely have a picture of a tornado?

A Chapter 2   C Chapter 6

B Chapter 5   D Chapter 7

2 Where should you begin reading to find out what kind of weather to expect if stratus clouds appear in the sky?

J Page 29

K Page 62

L Page 87

M Page 112

3 Chapter 6 would tell you most about

A the different layers of the atmosphere.

B how the weather affects our lives.

C the highest and lowest recorded temperatures around the world.

D using weather balloons to observe the weather.

STOP

Answers
S1 Ⓐ ● Ⓒ Ⓓ   2 Ⓙ Ⓚ ● Ⓜ
1 Ⓐ Ⓑ Ⓒ ●   3 Ⓐ Ⓑ Ⓒ ●

Level 9

61

Lesson 23: Using a Table of Contents

Study Skill: Using a table of contents to locate information

SAY: **Turn to Lesson 23, Using a Table of Contents, on page 61.**

Check to see that all students find Lesson 23.

SAY: **In Lesson 23 you will practice using a table of contents.**

Read the Directions to students.

SAY: **Now look at Try This.**

Read Try This to students.

SAY: **Study the sample table of contents. Now look at S1. Read the question and the answer choices carefully. Then darken the circle for the page on which Chapter 2 begins.**

Allow students time to choose and mark their answer.

SAY: **Now look at Think It Through.**

Read Think It Through to students. Check to see that all students have filled in the correct answer space. Ask students if they have any question

SAY: **Now you will practice using the sample table of contents to answer more questions. Put your finger on number 1. Do numbers 1 through 3 just as we did S1. When you come to the word *STOP* at the bottom of the page, put your pencils down. You may now begin.**

Allow students time to choose and mark their answers.

Review the questions and answer choices with students. Discuss with th class why one answer is correct and the others are not correct. Also che to see that students have carefully filled in their answer spaces and have completely erased any stray marks.

Lesson 24: Using the Dictionary

Directions: Darken the circle for the correct answer.

> **TRY THIS**
>
> Notice that entry words in the dictionary are listed alphabetically. Each entry gives the pronunciation and the meaning of the word.

S1   The *e* in *creak* sounds like the *e* in

    A   calculate.   C   cluster.

    B   chef.   D   cathedral.

> **THINK IT THROUGH**
>
> The correct answer is D. The *e* in <u>cathedral</u> is the only *e* that has the same pronunciation symbol as the *e* in <u>creak</u>.

STOP

Cc

calculate (kal´ • kyə • lāt)
To plan or intend to do something

cathedral (kə • thē´ • drəl)
A large and important church

cavalry (kav´ • əl • rē)
A group of soldiers fighting on horseback or from tanks

A cathedral

chef (shef)
The head cook of a restaurant or hotel

cluster (klus´ • tər)
To grow or group together

creak (krēk)
A sqeaking sound

Pronunciation Key

a	at	o	hot	ů	pull
ā	ape	ō	old	û	turn
ä	far	ô	song	ch	chin
â	care	ô	fork	ng	sing
e	end	oi	oil	sh	shop
ē	me	ou	out	th	thin
i	it	u	up	th	this
ī	ice	ū	use	hw	white
î	pierce	ü	rule	zh	treasure

The ə symbol stands for the unstressed vowel heard in about, taken, pencil, lemon, and circus.

1   How should you spell the name of a large and important church?

    A   Cathedrol

    B   Cathedral

    C   Cothedral

    D   Cuthedral

2   Which word fits best in the sentence "Danny liked to cook so much he decided to become a _____"?

    J   cavalry

    K   chef

    L   creak

    M   cluster

3   How might grapes grow?

    A   In a cluster

    B   In a creak

    C   In a chef

    D   In a cavalry

STOP
Level 9

Answers
S1 Ⓐ Ⓑ Ⓒ ●   2 Ⓙ ● Ⓛ Ⓜ
1 Ⓐ ● Ⓒ Ⓓ   3 ● Ⓑ Ⓒ Ⓓ

62

Lesson 24: Using the Dictionary

Study Skills: Using a dictionary to determine spelling, pronunciation, and word meaning

SAY: **Turn to Lesson 24, Using the Dictionary, on page 62.**

Check to see that all students find Lesson 24.

SAY: **In Lesson 24 you will practice using a dictionary to find information about words.**

Read the Directions to students.

SAY: **Now look at Try This.**

Read Try This to students.

SAY: **Study the sample dictionary and the pronunciation key. Now look at S1. Read the question and the answer choices carefully. Darken the circle for the answer choice that has the same *e* sound as the *e* in *creak*.**

Allow students time to choose and mark their answer.

SAY: **Now look at Think It Through.**

Read Think It Through to students. Check to see that all students have filled in the correct answer space. Ask students if they have any questions.

SAY: **Now you will practice using the sample dictionary to find more information. Put your finger on number 1. Do numbers 1 through 3 just as we did S1. When you come to the word *STOP* at the bottom of the page, put your pencils down. You may now begin.**

Allow students time to choose and mark their answers.

Review the questions and answer choices with students. Discuss with the class why one answer is correct and the others are not correct. Also check to see that students have carefully filled in their answer spaces and have completely erased any stray marks.

Lesson 25: Using the Library

Directions: Darken the circle for the correct answer.

> **TRY THIS** Think about the kind of information you are looking for. Then decide on the best place to find that information.

S1 Which drawer should you use to find the book *Nate the Great*?

   A Drawer F–G

   B Drawer M–N

   C Drawer S–T

   D Drawer U–V

> **THINK IT THROUGH** The correct answer is B. The title of the book begins with n, so you should use the drawer that has n on the label.

STOP

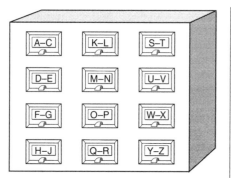

1 Which of the drawers should you use to find books about sports by Alan Woo?

   A Drawer A–C

   B Drawer D–E

   C Drawer S–T

   D Drawer W–X

2 Which of the drawers should you use to find a book about using rockets to carry missiles, travel in space, and shoot fireworks into the sky?

   J Drawer F–G

   K Drawer M–N

   L Drawer Q–R

   M Drawer S–T

3 Which of the drawers should you use to find books about different kinds of paints and how they are made?

   A Drawer D–E

   B Drawer H–J

   C Drawer M–N

   D Drawer O–P

GO ON

Answers
S1 Ⓐ ● Ⓒ Ⓓ   2 Ⓙ Ⓚ ● Ⓜ
1 Ⓐ Ⓑ Ⓒ ●   3 Ⓐ Ⓑ Ⓒ ●

Lesson 25: Using the Library

Study Skills: Using a card catalog; choosing appropriate reference materials to gather information

SAY: **Turn to Lesson 25, Using the Library, on page 63.**

Check to see that all students find Lesson 25.

SAY: **In Lesson 25 you will practice answering questions about using the library.**

Read the Directions to students.

SAY: **Now look at Try This.**

Read Try This to students.

SAY: **The sample card catalog on this page contains author, title, and subject cards that are arranged in alphabetical order. Study the sample card catalog. Now look at S1. Read the question and the answer choices carefully. Then darken the circle for the choice that tells which drawer you should use to find the book *Nate the Great*.**

Allow students time to choose and mark their answer.

SAY: **Now look at Think It Through.**

Read Think It Through to students. Check to see that all students have filled in the correct answer space. Ask students if they have any question

4 Which of these books would tell what a sentence is?

J An atlas

K A language book

L A social studies book

M A math book

5 Which of these would you find in an encyclopedia?

A A list of the cities in Texas

B A list of streets in your city

C A story about a neighborhood

D The meaning of the word *state*

6 Which of these would you probably find on a library shelf labeled *Health*?

J A book about sharks

K A book about childhood diseases

L A book about different kinds of music

M A book about learning to speak Spanish

7 Where in a book should you look to find out how many chapters are in it?

A In the index

B In the glossary

C On the title page

D In the table of contents

8 Which of these would you find in a dictionary?

J How to say the word *fjord*

K A map of the fjords in Norway

L A story about a girl who collected pictures of fjords

M A story about different kinds of fjords

9 Which section of the library would have a book about famous artists?

A Travel   C Health

B Biography   D Sports

10 Which of these books would show the states in the United States?

J A dictionary

K A language book

L A math book

M An atlas

STOP

Level 9

Answers

4 ⓙ ● ⓛ ⓜ   6 ⓙ ● ⓛ ⓜ   8 ● ⓚ ⓛ ⓜ   10 ⓙ ⓚ ⓛ ●

5 ● ⓑ ⓒ ⓓ   7 ⓐ ⓑ ⓒ ●   9 ⓐ ● ⓒ ⓓ

Allow students time to choose and mark their answers.

Review the questions and answer choices with students. Discuss with the class why one answer is correct and the others are not correct. Also check to see that students have carefully filled in their answer spaces and have completely erased any stray marks.

Unit 9 Test

━━━━━━━━━━ Unit 9 Test ━━━━━━━━━━

S1 A wrinkle

B youngster

C venture

D zoo

─────────────────────────── **STOP**

For questions 1–22, darken the circle for the correct answer.

For questions 1–8, choose the word or name that would come first if the words in each group were put in alphabetical order.

1 A ham

B gallon

C island

D fable

2 J Davis, Shenika

K Chang, Darice

L Gil, Esther

M Brown, Louis

3 A rodeo

B phone

C sauce

D quack

4 J thread

K throw

L thrash

M thrift

5 A Li, Jun

B Li, Ted

C Li, Qin

D Li, Eddie

6 J blackout

K blackbird

L blacksmith

M blackmail

7 A lower

B name

C kitten

D magic

8 J Rivera, Lucas

K Rivada, Kristyn

L Riviere, Robert

M Rivor, Robin

GO ON

Level 9

Answers

S1 Ⓐ Ⓑ ● Ⓓ   2 Ⓙ Ⓚ Ⓛ ●   4 Ⓙ Ⓚ ● Ⓜ   6 Ⓙ ● Ⓛ Ⓜ   8 Ⓙ ● Ⓛ Ⓜ

1 Ⓐ Ⓑ Ⓒ ●   3 Ⓐ ● Ⓒ Ⓓ   5 Ⓐ Ⓑ Ⓒ ●   7 Ⓐ Ⓑ ● Ⓓ

65

Unit 9 Test

SAY: **Turn to the Unit 9 Test on page 65.**

Check to see that all students find the Unit 9 Test.

SAY: **In this test you will use the study skills that we have practiced in this unit. Look at S1. Which word would come first if these words were put in alphabetical order? Darken the circle for the correct answer.**

Allow students time to choose and mark their answer.

SAY: **You should have darkened the circle for choice C. Venture would come before *wrinkle*, *youngster*, and *zoo*.**

Check to see that all students have filled in the correct answer space. Ask students if they have any questions.

SAY: **Now you will finish the test on your own. Read the directions carefully. Put your finger on number 1. Do numbers 1 through 22 just as we did S1. Read the questions and the answer choices carefully. Darken the circle for each correct answer. When you come to the words *GO ON* at the bottom of a page, continue working on the next page. When you come to the word *STOP* at the bottom of page 68, put your pencils down. You may now begin.**

Allow students time to choose and mark their answers.

Use the table of contents shown here to answer questions 9–13.

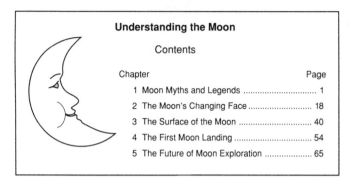

Understanding the Moon

Contents

9 Where should you begin reading to find out the sizes of craters on the moon's surface?

A Page 18

C Page 54

B Page 40

D Page 65

10 Which chapter would most likely have a picture of the first astronaut to set foot on the moon?

J Chapter 1

L Chapter 3

K Chapter 2

M Chapter 4

11 Chapter 2 would tell you most about

A the *Apollo II* spacecraft.

B mountains on the moon.

C how the moon was formed.

D a full moon.

12 Chapter 1 would tell you most about

J why ancient people worshiped the moon.

K scientific experiments on the moon.

L how the moon causes tides to change.

M when the next moon landing may be.

13 Which chapter might tell about plans for farming on the moon in the year 2222?

A Chapter 2

B Chapter 3

C Chapter 4

D Chapter 5

GO ON

Answers

9 Ⓐ ● Ⓒ Ⓓ   11 Ⓐ Ⓑ Ⓒ ●   13 Ⓐ Ⓑ Ⓒ ●

10 Ⓙ Ⓚ Ⓛ ●   12 ● Ⓚ Ⓛ Ⓜ

Use the dictionary and the pronunciation key shown here to answer questions 14–17.

fate (fāt)
What finally happens to someone or something

fathom (fath′ • əm)
A measure of length equal to six feet

feat (fēt)
An act or deed that shows great courage, strength, or skill

fiber (fi′ • bər)
A long, thin piece of material

A fiber

flee (flē)
To run away

focus (fo′ • kəs)
To make a clear picture

forbid (fər • bid′)
To order not to do something

frolic (frol′ • ik)
To play about happily

furrow (fûr′ • ō)
A long, narrow cut or dent

A furrow

Pronunciation Key

a	at	o	hot	u̇	pull	
ā	ape	ō	old	û	turn	
ä	far	ô	song	ch	chin	
â	care	ô	fork	ng	sing	
e	end	oi	oil	sh	shop	
ē	me	ou	out	th	thin	
i	it	u	up	th	this	
ī	ice	ū	use	hw	white	
î	pierce	ü	rule	zh	treasure	

The ə symbol stands for the unstressed vowel heard in **a**bout, tak**e**n, penc**i**l, lem**o**n, and circ**u**s.

14 How should you spell the name of a cut or dent in the mud?

J Farrow

K Ferrow

L Forrow

M Furrow

15 Which word fits best in the sentence "Jason's fate was to perform a great _____"?

A fiber

B feat

C furrow

D frolic

16 What might you do if a huge bear started to chase you?

J Forbid it

K Flee it

L Fiber it

M Focus it

17 The *o* in *focus* sounds like the *o* in

A furrow.

B forbid.

C frolic.

D fathom.

GO ON

Level 9

Answers
14 Ⓙ Ⓚ Ⓛ ●   16 Ⓙ ● Ⓛ Ⓜ
15 Ⓐ ● Ⓒ Ⓓ   17 ● Ⓑ Ⓒ Ⓓ

67

This card catalog contains author, title, and subject cards that are arranged in alphabetical order. Use the card catalog to answer questions 18–19.

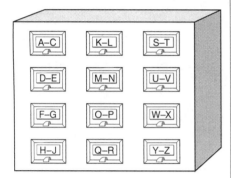

18 Which of the drawers should you use to find books about using computers in schools, businesses, and homes?

J Drawer A–C

K Drawer F–G

L Drawer H–J

M Drawer U–V

19 Which of the drawers should you use to find books about how shells are formed and where they are found?

A Drawer F–G

B Drawer H–J

C Drawer S–T

D Drawer W–X

For questions 20–22, choose the best place to find the information.

20 Which section of the library would have a book about Yellowstone National Park?

J Sports

K Travel

L Health

M Biography

21 Which of these books would show the cities, towns, and villages in Canada?

A An atlas

B A dictionary

C A language book

D A science book

22 For which of these should you use an encyclopedia?

J To find poems about Idaho

K To find the best way to go to Idaho from your town or city

L To learn what the state flower of Idaho is

M To learn how to write a book report about Idaho

STOP

Level 9

Answers

18 ● Ⓚ Ⓛ Ⓜ   20 Ⓙ ● Ⓛ Ⓜ   22 Ⓙ Ⓚ ● Ⓜ

68   19 Ⓐ Ⓑ ● Ⓓ   21 ● Ⓑ Ⓒ Ⓓ

SAY: **It is now time to stop. You have completed the Unit 9 Test. Make sure you have carefully filled in your answer spaces and have completely erased any stray marks. Then put your pencils down.**

After the test has been scored, review the questions and answer choices with students. If students are having difficulty, provide them with additional practice.

Test Best Comprehensive Tests

Getting Ready for the Comprehensive Tests

The Comprehensive Tests are designed to simulate the Iowa Tests of Basic Skills. Each Comprehensive Test has a recommended time limit. It is suggested that you follow these time limits and that you schedule no more than three tests in one day, providing sufficient breaks between tests.

Following the suggestions presented here will enable students to experience test taking under the same structured conditions that apply when achievement tests are administered. Furthermore, students will have a final opportunity to apply the skills they have learned in *Test Best*, prior to taking the Iowa Tests of Basic Skills.

The following table lists recommended test sessions and time limits for each test. It is suggested that you allow 15 or 20 minutes for students to complete the personal information required on the *Test Best* Answer Sheet shown on pages 81 and 82 of this book and on pages 93 and 94 of the student book.

Test Session	Comprehensive Test	Time Limit in Minutes
First Day	1—Vocabulary	5
	2—Reading Comprehension	15
	3—Spelling	10
Second Day	4—Language Skills	20
	5—Math Concepts and Estimation	20
	6—Math Problems	15
Third Day	7—Math Computation	10
	8—Maps and Diagrams	15
	9—Reference Materials	20

Test Day

To simulate the structured atmosphere of the Iowa Tests of Basic Skills, take the following steps on the day of the test:

- Hang a "Do Not Disturb—Testing" sign on the classroom door to avoid interruptions.

- Use a stopwatch to accurately observe the time limit marked on each test.

- Remove the Answer Sheet (found on pages 93 and 94) from each *Test Best on the Iowa Tests of Basic Skills* book.

- Seat students at an appropriate distance from one another and make sure that their desks are clear of all materials.

- Provide students with sharpened pencils that have erasers.

- Keep supplies, such as extra pencils and scratch paper for Tests 5, 6, and 7, readily available.

- Distribute the *Test Best* books to students and encourage them to do their best.

Before you begin, remind students to press firmly with their pencils make a dark mark. Remind students of the importance of completely filling in the answer spaces and erasing any stray marks that might be picked up as answers by the scoring machines.

While you are administering the Comprehensive Tests, make sure that students understand the directions before proceeding with each test. Circulate around the classroom, making sure that students are following the directions, that they are working on the appropriate test and that they are marking their Answer Sheet properly. Check to see that students have carefully filled in the answer spaces and have completely erased any stray marks.

Answer Sheet

Iowa Tests of Basic Skills is a trademark of the Riverside Publishing Company. Such company has neither endorsed nor authorized this test-preparation book.

STUDENT'S NAME

LAST · FIRST · MI

SCHOOL:
TEACHER:
FEMALE ○   MALE ○

BIRTH DATE

MONTH		DAY		YEAR	
Jan ○		⓪	⓪	⓪	⓪
Feb ○		①	①	①	①
Mar ○		②	②	②	②
Apr ○		③	③	③	③
May ○			④	④	④
Jun ○			⑤	⑤	⑤
Jul ○			⑥	⑥	⑥
Aug ○			⑦	⑦	⑦
Sep ○			⑧	⑧	⑧
Oct ○			⑨	⑨	⑨
Nov ○					
Dec ○					

GRADE ③ ④ ⑤ ⑥ ⑦ ⑧

TEST BEST
ON THE
IOWA TESTS OF BASIC SKILLS®

STECK-VAUGHN
COMPANY

TEST 1   Vocabulary

S1 ● Ⓑ Ⓒ Ⓓ   2 Ⓙ Ⓚ Ⓛ ●   4 Ⓙ Ⓚ Ⓛ ●   6 ● Ⓚ Ⓛ Ⓜ
1 Ⓐ Ⓑ Ⓒ ●   3 Ⓐ ● Ⓒ Ⓓ   5 Ⓐ Ⓑ ● Ⓓ   7 Ⓐ ● Ⓒ Ⓓ

TEST 2   Reading Comprehension

S1 ● Ⓑ Ⓒ Ⓓ   3 Ⓐ ● Ⓒ Ⓓ   6 ● Ⓚ Ⓛ Ⓜ   9 ● Ⓑ Ⓒ Ⓓ   12 Ⓙ ● Ⓛ Ⓜ   15 Ⓐ Ⓑ Ⓒ ●
1 ● Ⓑ Ⓒ Ⓓ   4 Ⓙ Ⓚ Ⓛ ●   7 Ⓐ Ⓑ ● Ⓓ   10 Ⓙ Ⓚ ● Ⓜ   13 Ⓐ Ⓑ ● Ⓓ
2 Ⓙ Ⓚ ● Ⓜ   5 Ⓐ Ⓑ Ⓒ ●   8 Ⓙ ● Ⓛ Ⓜ   11 Ⓐ Ⓑ Ⓒ ●   14 ● Ⓚ Ⓛ Ⓜ

TEST 3   Spelling

S1 Ⓐ Ⓑ ● Ⓓ Ⓔ   2 Ⓙ Ⓚ Ⓛ ● Ⓝ   4 Ⓙ Ⓚ Ⓛ Ⓜ ●   6 Ⓙ ● Ⓛ Ⓜ Ⓝ
1 Ⓐ Ⓑ Ⓒ Ⓓ ●   3 Ⓐ Ⓑ Ⓒ ● Ⓔ   5 ● Ⓑ Ⓒ Ⓓ Ⓔ   7 Ⓐ Ⓑ Ⓒ Ⓓ ●

Preparing the *Test Best* Answer Sheet

Distribute a *Test Best* Answer Sheet to each student. Refer to the *Test Best* Answer Sheet shown on this page and have students complete the required personal data. Use the procedures below to have students properly mark the personal data on the Answer Sheet. This will help ensure that students' test results will be properly recorded.

SAY: **Before we begin with Test 1 of the Comprehensive Tests, we need to complete some information on the *Test Best* Answer Sheet. We will do this together now. Make sure that you are looking at page 93, with the heading *STUDENT'S NAME* at the top of the page. Just below this at the left is the heading *LAST*. In the boxes under *LAST*, print your last name—one letter in each box. Print as many letters as will fit. In the boxes under *FIRST*, print your first name—one letter in each box. Print as many letters as will fit. If you have a middle name, print your middle initial in the *MI* box. Leave the *MI* box empty if you do not have a middle name.**

Allow students time to print their names.

SAY: **Now look at the columns of letters below each of the boxes. In each column, darken the circle that matches the letter in that box. Darken the empty circle at the top of the column if there is no letter in the box.**

Allow students time to darken the circles. Circulate around the classroom to make sure that students are completing the appropriate part of the Answer Sheet.

SAY: **Now look at the top right side of your Answer Sheet where it lists *SCHOOL* and *TEACHER*.**

Print the school's and your name on the chalkboard and allow students time to copy this information onto their Answer Sheets.

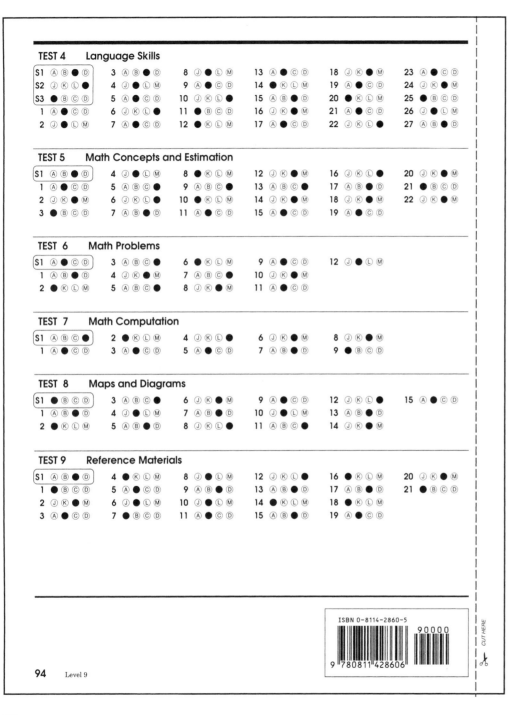

CUT HERE

SAY: **Now look at the section directly below *TEACHER*. Darken the circle for *FEMALE* if you are a girl. Darken the circle for *MAL[...]* if you are a boy. Then look at the *BIRTH DATE* section. Unde[...] *MONTH*, darken the circle for the month you were born. Und[...] *DAY*, darken the circles that have the one or two numerals [...] the day you were born. If your birthday has only one numera[...] darken the circle for zero in the first column of numerals. Under *YEAR*, darken the circles for the last two numbers of t[...] year you were born. Finally, under *GRADE*, darken the circle that has the number for your grade.**

Allow students time to complete the information. Remind students to pre[...] firmly on their pencils to make a dark mark. Check to see that students have carefully filled in the circles and have completely erased any stray marks. Remind students of the importance of completely filling the answ[...] space and erasing any stray marks that might be picked up as answers [...] the scoring machines.

ISBN 0-8114-2860-5

90000

9 780811 428606

S1 Purchased gifts

A bought

B wrapped

C received

D gave

STOP

For questions 1–7, darken the circle for the word or words that have the <u>same</u> or <u>almost the same</u> meaning as the word in dark type.

1 **Injure** your eye

A blink

B rub

C close

D hurt

2 **Disturb** the baby

J see

K hold

L rock

M upset

3 A **powerful** king

A kind

B strong

C rich

D cruel

4 The **price** of the dress

J size

K color

L style

M cost

5 **Obey** the rules

A say

B hear

C follow

D break

6 **Weep** loudly

J cry

K yell

L laugh

M sing

7 **Gradually** fill the glass

A quickly

B slowly

C carefully

D easily

STOP

Level 9

69

Comprehensive Tests

Test 1: Vocabulary

Allow 5 minutes for this test.

SAY: **Turn to Test 1, Vocabulary, on page 69.**

Check to see that all students find Test 1.

SAY: **In this test you will use your vocabulary skills to answer questions. Look at S1. Read the phrase and the answer choices silently. Then darken the circle for the correct answer.**

Allow students time to choose and mark their answer.

SAY: **You should have darkened the circle for choice *A*. The word *bought* has the same meaning as the word in dark type, *purchased*.**

Check to see that all students have filled in the correct answer space. Ask students if they have any questions.

SAY: **Now you will finish the test on your own. Read the directions carefully. Put your finger on number 1. Do numbers 1 through 7 just as we did S1. Darken the circle for each correct answer. When you come to the word *STOP* at the bottom of the page, put your pencils down. You have 5 minutes to complete the test. You may now begin.**

Allow students 5 minutes to choose and mark their answers.

SAY: **It is now time to stop. You have completed Test 1. Make sure you have carefully filled in your answer spaces and have completely erased any stray marks. Then put your pencils down and close your books.**

After the test has been scored, review the questions and answer choices with students. If students are having difficulty, provide them with additional practice.

S1 Joe was hungry. He took bread, ham, and cheese from the refrigerator. He laid everything on the table. Then he realized he had forgotten something. He went back to the refrigerator and took out a big jar of mustard.

What was Joe making?

A   A sandwich

B   A fruit salad

C   Macaroni and cheese

D   A hamburger

STOP

For questions 1–15, darken the circle for the correct answer.

> Many brightly colored lights are made from a gas called neon. About eighty years ago, Georges Claude, a French chemist, found a way to use neon to make lights. He took the air out of a glass tube and replaced it with neon. When electricity was passed through the neon, a colorful light was created.
>
> You have probably seen neon lights in restaurant signs or on highways. Airports sometimes use neon lights to guide airplanes because neon can be seen through thick fog. Today some people use neon signs in their homes and offices. Some works of art in museums are made of neon lights.
>
> Argon is another gas used in signs. It gives off the color lavender. Neon gives off an orange-red color. Even though different gases are used, people always call the signs neon signs.

1   What is neon?

A   A gas   C   A planet

B   A sign   D   A color

2   Why are neon lights used at airports?

J   They are colorful.

K   They are in the air.

L   They can be seen through fog.

M   They can be seen at any time of day or night.

3   What must be taken out of the glass tube before neon is put in?

A   Electricity   C   Fog

B   Air   D   Argon

4   How is argon different from neon?

J   It is a gas.

K   It is not used in signs.

L   It is found only in works of art.

M   It gives off the color lavender.

GO ON

Level 9

Test 2: Reading Comprehension

Allow 15 minutes for this test.

SAY: **Turn to Test 2, Reading Comprehension, on page 70.**

Check to see that all students find Test 2.

SAY: **In this test you will use your reading skills to answer question about selections that you read. Look at S1. Read the selection the question, and the answer choices silently. Then darken the circle for the correct answer.**

Allow students time to choose and mark their answer.

SAY: **You should have darkened the circle for choice A. Joe is usin the bread, ham, cheese, and mustard to make a sandwich.**

Check to see that all students have filled in the correct answer space. Ask students if they have any questions.

SAY: **Now you will finish the test on your own. Read the directions carefully. Now put your finger on number 1. Do numbers 1 through 15 just as we did S1. Darken the circle for each correct answer. When you come to the words GO ON at the bottom of a page, continue working on the next page. When you come to the word STOP at the bottom of page 73, put your pencils down. You have 15 minutes to complete the test. You may now begin.**

Allow students 15 minutes to choose and mark their answers.

In this story a family has spent a long day traveling to a new home.

The January wind blew icy cold across the prairie. Carrie and I huddled together in the wagon, trying to stay warm. Soon Father would stop to make camp for the night. Then we could build a fire to warm our fingers and toes. We watched Mother. She was swaying with the motion of the wagon as she mended our clothes. When we reached our new home on the frontier, there would be no place to buy new things. We would have to make do with what we had. That seemed both scary and exciting to us.

Suddenly I heard Father shout, "John, quick! Come up here and look at this!" I hurried to the front of the wagon and looked out on a large herd of buffalo. The powerful animals with brown shaggy coats moved slowly toward the south. They kept their backs to the wind, which blew colder as the day went on.

"This might be a good stopping place. It looks like we might be in for some bad weather," said Father. Clouds were gathering in the north as we prepared for the night. I helped Father look for dried brush to start a fire. Carrie and Mother made preparations for dinner. We all worked quickly, sensing that we had a long, hard night ahead.

5   **During which season is this story set?**

A   Spring   C   Fall

B   Summer   D   Winter

6   **The family was traveling in**

J   a covered wagon.

K   a train.

L   a boat.

M   a stagecoach.

7   **How did the family members probably feel as they prepared for the night?**

A   Excited

B   Playful

C   Cautious

D   Relaxed

8   **Who is telling this story?**

J   Carrie

K   John

L   Mother

M   Father

GO ON

When Jane Goodall was a young girl, she liked to watch animals. She learned many things about animals by watching them eat, sleep, and play. When she was older, Jane went to Africa to study wild chimpanzees. She had to live in the jungle to be near the chimpanzees all of the time. It was hard for Jane at first. The chimpanzees ran whenever she came near. But soon they were more comfortable when she was around. They let her watch them. She learned how they collected vines and made them into beds in the tops of trees. She found that they greeted each other with noises and hugs. Jane also found that the chimpanzees used tools. They poked grass into the dirt to find bugs to eat.

9   **Why did the chimpanzees run from Jane at first?**

  A They were scared of her.

  B They were playing hide-and-seek.

  C They were racing each other.

  D They were looking for food.

10   **Why did the chimpanzees collect vines?**

  J To eat

  K To swing from

  L To make a bed

  M To hide from Jane

11   **What tool did the chimpanzees use?**

  A Dirt

  B Bugs

  C Vines

  D Grass

12   **What is this passage mainly about?**

  J Wild chimpanzees and how they live

  K Jane Goodall's study of chimpanzees

  L Foods chimpanzees eat

  M Jane Goodall's life

GO ON

Level 9

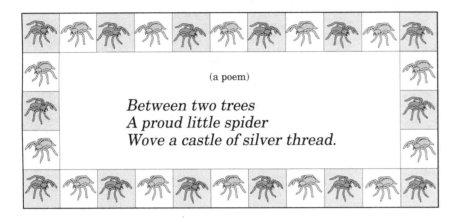

(a poem)

Between two trees
A proud little spider
Wove a castle of silver thread.

13 In this poem, what is the castle of silver thread?

    A A house

    B A curtain

    C A web

    D A sweater

14 In this poem, why is the spider "proud"?

    J She has woven a beautiful web.

    K She knows much about trees.

    L She has many legs.

    M She has made friends with a bee.

15 Which picture shows the spider in this poem?

A

B

C

D

STOP

Level 9

73

SAY: **It is now time to stop. You have completed Test 2. Make sure you have carefully filled in your answer spaces and have completely erased any stray marks. Then put your pencils down.**

After the test has been scored, review the questions and answer choices with students. If students are having difficulty, provide them with additional practice.

Test 3: Spelling

S1
A blew
B ride
C stormey
D bread
E (No mistakes)

STOP

For questions 1–7, darken the circle for the word that is <u>not</u> spelled correctly. Darken the circle for *No mistakes* if there are <u>no</u> spelling errors.

1
A stick
B lake
C race
D cost
E (No mistakes)

2
J badge
K does
L bump
M boxs
N (No mistakes)

3
A magic
B spoil
C forty
D offen
E (No mistakes)

4
J closed
K marches
L running
M ladies
N (No mistakes)

5
A nife
B sight
C nose
D grin
E (No mistakes)

6
J jewel
K shovle
L animal
M lovely
N (No mistakes)

7
A ladder
B agree
C honor
D rubber
E (No mistakes)

STOP

Level 9

Test 3: Spelling

Allow 10 minutes for this test.

SAY: **Turn to Test 3, Spelling, on page 74.**

Check to see that all students find Test 3.

SAY: **In this test you will use your language skills to find spelling mistakes. Look at S1. Read the answer choices carefully. Then darken the circle for the word that has a spelling mistake. Darken the circle for *No mistakes* if there is no spelling error.**

Allow students time to choose and mark their answer.

SAY: **You should have darkened the circle for choice *C* because it shows a mistake in the spelling of *stormy*. The correct spellin of *stormy* is *s-t-o-r-m-y*.**

Check to see that all students have filled in the correct answer space. Ask students if they have any questions.

SAY: **Now you will finish the test on your own. Read the directions carefully. Put your finger on number 1. Do numbers 1 through just as we did S1. Darken the circle for each correct answer. When you come to the word *STOP* at the bottom of the page, put your pencils down. You have 10 minutes to complete the test. You may now begin.**

Allow students 10 minutes to choose and mark their answers.

SAY: **It is now time to stop. You have completed Test 3. Make sure you have carefully filled in your answer spaces and have completely erased any stray marks. Then put your pencils down.**

After the test has been scored, review the questions and answer choices with students. If students are having difficulty, provide them with additional practice.

Test 4: Language Skills

S1
- A During the summer there is a
- B craft fair in our town on the third
- C saturday of every month.
- D *(No mistakes)*

STOP

S2
- J Mrs. Kato has two dogs.
- K Their names are Chip and Big.
- L She walks them every day.
- M *(No mistakes)*

STOP

S3
- A We made these here pillows.
- B The feathers came from my
- C grandmother's geese.
- D *(No mistakes)*

STOP

For questions 1–7, darken the circle for the line that has a capitalization error. Darken the circle for *No mistakes* if there is no error.

1
- A Mother said that I could not
- B play after school because i'm
- C going to the doctor's office.
- D *(No mistakes)*

2
- J At the school plant sale,
- K Masako bought an african
- L violet for her math teacher.
- M *(No mistakes)*

3
- A Kevin has a big black dog that
- B loves to swim in the lake.
- C Kevin named his dog coal.
- D *(No mistakes)*

4
- J Terry wants to go camping
- K in june. The park gets too
- L crowded later in the summer.
- M *(No mistakes)*

5
- A 304 Great West Road
- B clovis, NM 64132
- C November 3, 1995
- D *(No mistakes)*

6
- J Dear Robert,
- K Congratulations on winning
- L your first fishing tournament.
- M *(No mistakes)*

7
- A I wish I could have been there!
- B sincerely yours,
- C Rodrigo
- D *(No mistakes)*

Test 4: Language Skills

Allow 20 minutes for this test.

SAY: **Turn to Test 4, Language Skills, on page 75.**

Check to see that all students find Test 4.

SAY: **In this test you will use your language skills to answer questions. Look at S1. Read the sentence. Then darken the circle for the line that has an error in capitalization. Darken the circle for *No mistakes* if there is no error.**

Allow students time to choose and mark their answer.

SAY: **You should have darkened the circle for choice *C*. The word *Saturday* should be capitalized because it is a proper noun.**

Check to see that all students have filled in the correct answer space. Ask students if they have any questions.

SAY: **Now look at S2. Read the sentences. Then darken the circle for the line that has an error in punctuation. Darken the circle for *No mistakes* if there is no error.**

Allow students time to choose and mark their answer.

SAY: **You should have darkened the circle for choice *M*. None of the lines has an error in punctuation.**

Check to see that all students have filled in the correct answer space. Ask students if they have any questions.

SAY: **Now look at S3. Read the sentences. Then darken the circle for the line that has an error in the way the words are used. Darken the circle for *No mistakes* if there is no error.**

Allow students time to choose and mark their answer.

SAY: **You should have darkened the circle for choice *A*. The word *here* should not be in the first sentence.**

Check to see that all students have filled in the correct answer space. Ask students if they have any questions.

Test 4: Language Skills

S1
  A During the summer there is a
  B craft fair in our town on the third
  C saturday of every month.
  D *(No mistakes)*

— **STOP**

S2
  J Mrs. Kato has two dogs.
  K Their names are Chip and Big.
  L She walks them every day.
  M *(No mistakes)*

— **STOP**

S3
  A We made these here pillows.
  B The feathers came from my
  C grandmother's geese.
  D *(No mistakes)*

— **STOP**

For questions 1–7, darken the circle for the line that has a capitalization error. Darken the circle for *No mistakes* if there is no error.

1
  A Mother said that I could not
  B play after school because i'm
  C going to the doctor's office.
  D *(No mistakes)*

2
  J At the school plant sale,
  K Masako bought an african
  L violet for her math teacher.
  M *(No mistakes)*

3
  A Kevin has a big black dog that
  B loves to swim in the lake.
  C Kevin named his dog coal.
  D *(No mistakes)*

4
  J Terry wants to go camping
  K in june. The park gets too
  L crowded later in the summer.
  M *(No mistakes)*

5
  A 304 Great West Road
  B clovis, NM 64132
  C November 3, 1995
  D *(No mistakes)*

6
  J Dear Robert,
  K Congratulations on winning
  L your first fishing tournament.
  M *(No mistakes)*

7
  A I wish I could have been there!
  B sincerely yours,
  C Rodrigo
  D *(No mistakes)*

GO ON

Level 9

75

SAY: **Now you will finish the test on your own. Read the directions carefully. Put your finger on number 1. Do numbers 1 through 27 just as we did the samples. Darken the circle for each correct answer. When you come to the words *GO ON* at the bottom of a page, continue working on the next page. When you come to the word *STOP* at the bottom of page 78, put your pencils down. You have 20 minutes to complete the test. You may now begin.**

Allow students 20 minutes to choose and mark their answers.

For questions 8–12, darken the circle for the line that has a punctuation error. Darken the circle for *No mistakes* if there is no error.

8   J Corey lost one of his shoes.

      K If he doesnt find it soon, he

      L cannot play in the soccer game.

      M *(No mistakes)*

9   A Tina wanted to finish her

      B homework before 430 so she

      C could play with her friends.

      D *(No mistakes)*

10   J   925 Hallway Drive

      K   Sparta, NJ 07871

      L   December 2, 1995

      M *(No mistakes)*

11   A Dear Anthony

      B It snowed four inches today.

      C Mom and I made a big snowman.

      D *(No mistakes)*

12   J We miss you a lot

      K   Your brother,

      L   José

      M *(No mistakes)*

For questions 13–17, darken the circle for the line that has an error in the way the words are used. Darken the circle for *No mistakes* if there is no error.

13   A Last night my father took me

      B out to eat. I had the bestest

      C spaghetti I have ever eaten.

      D *(No mistakes)*

14   J The baby want a drink

      K of orange juice from that

      L cup on the table.

      M *(No mistakes)*

15   A Now where did Curtis and

      B Amy go? They must be around

      C here somewheres.

      D *(No mistakes)*

16   J Polly wanted to go to the

      K movies, but her mother

      L wouldn't give her no money.

      M *(No mistakes)*

17   A Anita hid behind a tree,

      B but Charlie finded her

      C before anyone else.

      D *(No mistakes)*

GO ON

Level 9

For questions 18–20, darken the circle for the word or words that will correct the underlined part of the sentence. Darken the circle for *No change* if there is no error.

18 Sam ran into the house **wherever** he heard a loud noise outside.

J although   K unless   L because   M *(No change)*

19 I **am** surprised to see that a goat had eaten all of the flowers in our yard.

A will be   B was   C have been   D *(No change)*

20 The wind blew the leaves **during** the air.

J into   K over   L against   M *(No change)*

For questions 21–23, darken the circle for the line that expresses the idea most clearly.

21 A Outside the children ran after school to play.

B After school the children ran outside to play.

C After school to play ran the children outside.

D The children ran to school after to play outside.

22 J Max borrows the newspaper. You want to read it after.

K The newspaper Max wants to borrow after you read it.

L After you read it, Max wants the newspaper to borrow.

M Max wants to borrow the newspaper after you read it.

23 A The neighborhood meeting Mr. Johnson missed last night.

B Mr. Johnson missed the neighborhood meeting last night.

C Last night the neighborhood meeting Mr. Johnson missed.

D The neighborhood Mr. Johnson missed was last night in the meeting.

GO ON

For questions 24–27, darken the circle for the correct answer.

> [1] Our neighborhood park is always full of people. [2] They should sell food there. [3] Older adults sit on the benches and read their newspapers early in the morning. [4] The slide and swings are a favorite place to play for the young children. [5] Mothers often walk their babies in strollers around the park. [6] Older children play baseball or basketball there.

24 Which is the best opening sentence for this paragraph?

J Parks are very crowded in the spring.

K I love to go to the park in the summer.

L Parks offer many things for many people.

M I play with the older kids at our park.

25 Which sentence does not belong in this paragraph?

A Sentence 2

B Sentence 3

C Sentence 4

D Sentence 5

> [1] One evening last summer we went to the Hillside Theater. [2] We brought a picnic and sat on a blanket on the lawn. [3] It is a large outdoor theater. [4] The people sitting next to us had small children that were very noisy. [5] The band performed on the evening we were there. [6] While we listened to the music, we looked up at the moon and stars.

26 Where does sentence 3 belong in this paragraph?

J Before sentence 1

K Between sentences 1 and 2

L Between sentences 4 and 5

M Where it is now

27 Which is the best ending sentence for this paragraph?

A My family and I like to go places together in the evening.

B Many musical instruments were used.

C Going to an outdoor concert at night was a special treat for us.

D Listening to music is an activity that my family enjoys.

STOP

Level 9

SAY: **It is now time to stop. You have completed Test 4. Make sure you have carefully filled in your answer spaces and have completely erased any stray marks. Then put your pencils down and close your books.**

After the test has been scored, review the questions and answer choices with students. If students are having difficulty, provide them with additional practice.

S1 Which of these sets is a group of even numbers?

   A 3, 6, 12

   B 2, 5, 9

   C 8, 14, 18

   D 1, 7, 11

                    STOP

For problems 1–22, darken the circle for the correct answer.

1 Which of the following numbers should go in the box?

   A 19

   B 21

   C 24

   D 25

2 Which of the following is another name for 732?

   J Seventy thirty two

   K Seven thousand thirty-two

   L Seven hundred thirty-two

   M Seventy hundred thirty-two

3 Which of the following numbers is greater than 62?

   A 74

   B 58

   C 47

   D 33

4 What fraction of the group of rectangles are shaded?

   J $\frac{1}{2}$

   K $\frac{1}{3}$

   L $\frac{2}{3}$

   M $\frac{3}{1}$

5 Roberto wants to buy a bookmark for 89¢. He has 2 quarters, 3 nickels, and 4 pennies. **How much more money does Roberto need?**

   A 70¢

   B 64¢

   C 21¢

   D 20¢

                      GO ON

Level 9

79

Test 5: Math Concepts and Estimation

Allow 20 minutes for this test.

Distribute scratch paper to students. Tell them that they may use the scratch paper to work only problems 1–16. They must work problems 17–2. in their head.

SAY: **Turn to Test 5, Math Concepts and Estimation, on page 79.**

Check to see that all students find Test 5.

SAY: **In this test you will use your mathematics skills to solve problems. Look at S1. Read the question and the answer choices carefully. Then darken the circle for the correct answer.**

Allow students time to choose and mark their answer.

SAY: **You should have darkened the circle for choice _C_ because _8_, _14_, and _18_ are a group of even numbers.**

Check to see that all students have filled in the correct answer space. Ask students if they have any questions.

SAY: **Now you will finish the test on your own. Read the directions carefully. Put your finger on number 1. Do numbers 1 through 2 just as we did S1. Darken the circle for each correct answer. When you come to the words _GO ON_ at the bottom of a page, continue working on the next page. When you come to the word _STOP_ at the bottom of page 82, put your pencils down. Remember that you may not use scratch paper for numbers 17–22. You have 20 minutes to complete the test. You may now begin.**

Allow students 20 minutes to choose and mark their answers.

6 Which is the correct way to write
400 + 90 + 3 as one numeral?

J 40,903

K 4093

L 1303

M 493

7 What numeral should go in the ☐
to make this number sentence correct?

$$6 + 5 + 7 = 5 + \square + 7$$

A 18

B 7

C 6

D 5

8 When he trains for the swim team,
Mark walks 6 blocks to the pool. He
swims 14 laps every morning and 27
laps every afternoon. **Which of these
number sentences shows how many
more laps Mark swims in the
afternoon than in the morning?**

J 27 − 14 = 13

K 14 − 6 = 8

L 27 + 14 = 41

M 27 − 14 − 6 = 7

9 What is the missing factor in this
number sentence?

$$32 \div \square = 4$$

A 128

B 28

C 36

D 8

10 Which is the best estimate of the
length of your thumb?

J Less than 6 inches

K Between 1 and 2 feet

L More than 24 inches

M Between 6 and 12 inches

11 Which sign should go in the ◯ in this
number sentence?

$$7 \bigcirc 3 = 21$$

A ÷

B ×

C +

D −

GO ON

12 What is the area of this shape in square units?

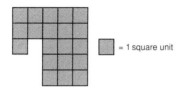 = 1 square unit

J 5 square units

K 17 square units

L 20 square units

M 25 square units

13 Which figure is made of all rectangles?

A

C

B

D

14 What shape was cut from the piece of folded paper shown here?

J ◯   L ◇

K ▷   M ▭

15 Which of these pictures shows a star inside a closed figure?

A

C

B

D

16 Taylor left for New York on July 15. She came home 2 weeks later. **What date did Taylor come home?**

J July 1

K July 17

L July 22

M July 29

17 Which is the closest estimate of the total cost of the books?

$5.95 $3.25 $7.75

A $5.00 + $3.00 + $8.00

B $6.00 + $3.00 + $7.00

C $6.00 + $3.00 + $8.00

D $6.00 + $4.00 + $8.00

18 Which is the closest estimate of 9 × 18?

J   Between 50 and 100

K   Between 100 and 150

L   Between 150 and 200

M   More than 200

19 Which is the closest estimate of 52 + 71?

A   Less than 120

B   Between 120 and 130

C   Between 130 and 140

D   More than 140

20 Which is the closest estimate of the total cost of the stamps?

29¢   73¢

J   80¢

K   90¢

L $1.00

M $1.10

21 The closest estimate of how much the bear has grown is _____.

Bear at birth   Bear now

11 inches   64 inches

A   50 inches   C   70 inches

B   60 inches   D   80 inches

22 The closest estimate of $567 – $218 is _____.

J $4

K $40

L $400

M $4000

STOP

Level 9

82

After the test has been scored, review the questions and answer choices with students. If students are having difficulty, provide them with additional practice.

Test 6: Math Problems

S1 Ms. Lenz has 24 students. On Tuesday 7 students were absent. **How many students were in Ms. Lenz's class on Tuesday?**

A 31

B 17

C 14

D Not given

— **STOP**

For questions 1–12, darken the circle for the correct answer. Darken the circle for <u>Not given</u> if the answer is <u>not</u> shown.

1 Maria had 3 hamsters. Each hamster had 7 babies. **How many baby hamsters did Maria have?**

A 4

B 10

C 21

D Not given

2 At the pet store, Maria sold 6 golden hamsters and 4 brown hamsters. Her brother sold a teddy bear hamster that weighed 3 ounces. **How many hamsters did they sell?**

J 11

K 13

L 14

M Not given

3 Maria came home from the pet store at 4:00. Her mother had gone to the grocery store. **Maria could find out how long her mother had been gone if she knew**

A what her mother went to buy.

B what time it would be when her mother got home.

C how far it was to the grocery store.

D what time her mother left.

Use the picture shown here to answer questions 4–6.

Circus Snacks

Popcorn
6 coupons

Hot Dog
8 coupons

Candy Apples
3 for 5 coupons

Lemonade
3 coupons

4 Marco wanted a hot dog, a glass of lemonade, and a box of popcorn. **How many coupons did he need?**

J 11

K 14

L 17

M Not given

5 **How many more coupons are needed for a hot dog than for a glass of lemonade?**

A 6

B 11

C 24

D Not given

6 Marco had 30 coupons. He used the same number of coupons each time he went to the snack bar. **What else do you need to know to find out how many times he went to the snack bar?**

J How many coupons he used each time he went

K How many boxes of popcorn he ate

L How much money the coupons cost

M How many times he went to the circus

— **GO ON**

Test 6: Math Problems

Allow 15 minutes for this test.

Distribute scratch paper to students. Tell them that they may use the scratch paper to work the problems.

SAY: **Turn to Test 6, Math Problems, on page 83.**

Check to see that all students find Test 6.

SAY: **In this test you will use your mathematics skills to solve problems. Look at S1. Read the problem and the answer choices carefully. Then darken the circle for the correct answer.**

Allow students time to choose and mark their answer.

SAY: **You should have darkened the circle for choice *B*. If Ms. Lenz has 24 students and 7 were absent on Tuesday, *17* students were in class that day.**

Check to see that all students have filled in the correct answer space. Ask students if they have any questions.

SAY: **Now you will finish the test on your own. Read the directions carefully. Put your finger on number 1. Do numbers 1 through 12 just as we did S1. Darken the circle for each correct answer. When you come to the words *GO ON* at the bottom of the page, continue working on the next page. When you come to the word *STOP* at the bottom of page 84, put your pencils down. You have 15 minutes to complete the test. You may now begin.**

Allow students 15 minutes to choose and mark their answers.

Use the table shown here to answer questions 7–9.

Birds Seen by Three Members of Smallville Bird Club

Kind of Bird	Dan	Julia	Sarah
Robin	8	9	6
Sparrow	6	14	8
Cardinal	13	7	15
Pigeon	12	12	12
Blue Jay	10	4	16

7   Each member of the bird club saw the same number of

A   robins.

B   sparrows.

C   cardinals.

D   pigeons.

8   How many sparrows did Julia see?

J   7

K   9

L   14

M   20

9   Sarah saw twice as many blue jays as

A   robins.

B   sparrows.

C   cardinals.

D   pigeons.

Use the graph shown here to answer questions 10–12.

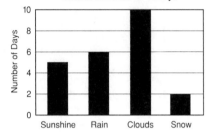

Weather in Dallas for 10 days

10   How many days did it rain?

J   1

K   5

L   6

M   10

11   How many more days had clouds than sunshine?

A   4   C   6

B   5   D   10

12   What can you conclude from this graph?

J   Dallas was rainy most of the time.

K   Dallas was rainy and cloudy most of the time.

L   Dallas had as many days of snow as it did rain.

M   Dallas was rainy and snowy most of the time.

STOP

Level 9

SAY: **It is now time to stop. You have completed Test 6. Make sure you have carefully filled in your answer spaces and have completely erased any stray marks. Then put your pencils down.**

After the test has been scored, review the questions and answer choices with students. If students are having difficulty, provide them with additional practice.

Test 7: Math Computation

━━━━ Test 7: Math Computation ━━━━

S1
$5 + 9 =$

A 12
B 13
C 45
D N

STOP

For problems 1–9, darken the circle for the correct answer. Darken the circle for <u>N</u> if the answer is <u>not</u> given.

1
191
$+ 123$

A 214
B 314
C 324
D N

2
$911 + 2 + 64 =$

J 977
K 1175
L 1553
M N

3
$82 - 73 =$

A 8
B 9
C 11
D N

4
975
$- 559$

J 326
K 426
L 1134
M N

5
$224 - 7 =$

A 207
B 217
C 291
D N

6
$6 \times 811 =$

J 817
K 4811
L 4866
M N

7
5000
$\times 5$

A 2500
B 5005
C 25,000
D N

8
$45 \div 5 =$

J 7
K 8
L 9
M N

9
$18 \div 6 =$

A 3
B 4
C 5
D N

STOP

Level 9

85

Test 7: Math Computation

Allow 10 minutes for this test.

Distribute scratch paper to students. Tell them that they may use the scratch paper to work the problems.

SAY: **Turn to Test 7, Math Computation, on page 85.**

Check to see that all students find Test 7.

SAY: **In this test you will use your mathematics skills to solve problems. Look at S1. Read the problem and the answer choices carefully. Then darken the circle for the correct answer. Darken the circle for *N* if the answer is not given.**

Allow students time to choose and mark their answer.

SAY: **You should have darkened the circle for choice *D* because *5 + 9 = 14*, and *14* is not given.**

Check to see that all students have filled in the correct answer space. Ask students if they have any questions.

SAY: **Now you will finish the test on your own. Read the directions carefully. Put your finger on number 1. Do numbers 1 through ! just as we did the sample. Read the problems and the answer choices carefully. Darken the circle for each correct answer. When you come to the word *STOP* at the bottom of the page, put your pencils down. You have 10 minutes to complete the test. You may now begin.**

Allow students 10 minutes to choose and mark their answers.

SAY: **It is now time to stop. You have completed Test 7. Make sure you have carefully filled in your answer spaces and have completely erased any stray marks. Then put your pencils down and close your books.**

After the test has been scored, review the questions and answer choices with students. If students are having difficulty, provide them with additional practice.

Test 8: Maps and Diagrams

S1

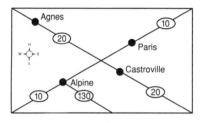

Through which two cities does Highway 10 pass?

A Paris and Alpine

B Castroville and Agnes

C Agnes and Alpine

D Paris and Agnes

STOP

For questions 1–15, darken the circle for the correct answer.

Use the map shown here to answer questions 1–4.

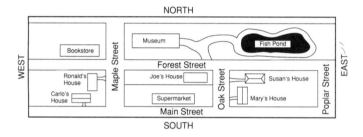

1 Where is the fish pond?

A West of Maple Street

B South of Susan's house

C North of Forest Street

D West of the museum

2 What is between Ronald's house and Joe's house?

J Maple Street

K Forest Street

L Carlo's house

M The supermarket

3 Which is farthest from Mary's house?

A Joe's house

B Susan's house

C The museum

D The bookstore

4 Susan walked from the museum to Forest Street. **In which direction did she go?**

J North   L East

K South   M West

GO ON

Level 9

Test 8: Maps and Diagrams

Allow 15 minutes for this test.

SAY: **Turn to Test 8, Maps and Diagrams, on page 86.**

Check to see that all students find Test 8.

SAY: **In this test you will use your map and diagram skills to answer questions. Look at S1. Study the map. Then read the question and the answer choices carefully. Darken the circle for the correct answer.**

Allow students time to choose and mark their answer.

SAY: **You should have darkened the circle for choice *A* because Highway 10 passes through Paris and Alpine.**

Check to see that all students have filled in the correct answer space. Ask students if they have any questions.

SAY: **Now you will finish the test on your own. Read the directions carefully. Put your finger on number 1. Do numbers 1 through 15 just as we did S1. Darken the circle for each correct answer. When you come to the words *GO ON* at the bottom of a page, continue working on the next page. When you come to the word *STOP* at the bottom of page 88, put your pencils down. You have 15 minutes to complete the test. You may now begin.**

Allow students 15 minutes to choose and mark their answers.

This map shows an imaginary country that has four states. Use the map to answer questions 5–7.

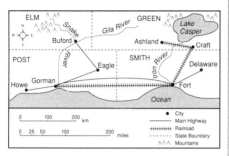

5   How would cotton that is grown around Ashland probably be shipped to Craft?

A   By truck

B   By bus

C   By railroad

D   By river barge

6   Which would be the shortest way to travel between Fort and Gorman?

J   By boat on the ocean

K   By highway through Delaware

L   By railroad

M   By boat down the Gila River

7   In which state is Eagle located?

A   Green   C   Post

B   Elm   D   Smith

Use the chart shown here to answer questions 8–10.

**Green Thumb Nursery Sales
(One Month)**

Vegetable Plants	○ ○ ○ ◖
Shrubs	🌿 🌿
Fruit Trees	🌳 🌳 🌳
Evergreen Trees	🌲 🌲 🌲 🌲 🌲
Flowering Plants	🪴 🪴 🪴 🪴 🪴 🪴
House Plants	🪴 🪴 🪴 🪴

Each complete picture = 10

8   How many evergreen trees did the Green Thumb Nursery sell?

J   15   L   35

K   30   M   45

9   How many more house plants than fruit trees were sold?

A   5

B   10

C   25

D   30

10   What kinds of plants added together equal the number of flowering plants sold by the nursery?

J   Vegetable plants and shrubs

K   Shrubs and house plants

L   Vegetable plants and fruit trees

M   Evergreen trees and house plants

GO ON

Level 9

87

Use the calendar shown here to answer questions 11–13.

JANUARY

Sun.	Mon.	Tues.	Wed.	Thurs.	Fri.	Sat.
				1	2	3
4	5	6	7	8	9	10
11	12	13	14	15	16	17
18	19	20	21	22	23	24
25	26	27	28	29	30	31

11   Matthew has a social studies test on January 16th. **What day is that?**

   A Tuesday   **C** Thursday

   B Wednesday   **D** Friday

12   Alissa's safety patrol club meets every Tuesday and Friday. **How many meetings will there be in the month of January?**

   J Six   **L** Eight

   K Seven   **M** Nine

13   Tessie gets her allowance on the third Friday of every month. **What date in January is that?**

   A The 2nd

   B The 9th

   C The 16th

   D The 23rd

This diagram shows how an automobile goes from being an idea to a product. Use the diagram to answer questions 14–15.

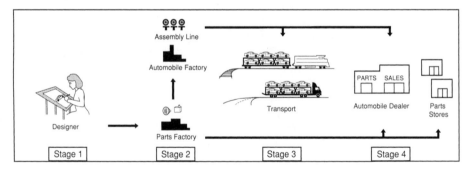

14   **What happens to car parts at the automobile factory?**

   J They are drawn.

   L They are sold to buyers.

   L They become cars.

   M They are shipped to dealers.

15   **Where do parts stores probably get automobile parts?**

   A From automobile dealers

   B From the parts factory

   C From the automobile factory

   D From the designer

STOP

Level 9

SAY: **It is now time to stop. You have completed Test 8. Make sure you have carefully filled in your answer spaces and have completely erased any stray marks. Then put your pencils down and close your books.**

After the test has been scored, review the questions and answer choices with students. If students are having difficulty, provide them with additional practice.

Test 9: Reference Materials

Allow 20 minutes for this test.

SAY: **Turn to Test 9, Reference Materials, on page 89.**

Check to see that all students find Test 9.

SAY: **In this test you will use your study skills to answer questions about reference materials. Look at S1. Darken the circle for the word that would come first if these words were put in alphabetical order.**

Allow students time to choose and mark their answer.

SAY: **You should have darkened the circle for choice *C. Its* would come before *jacket*, *knee*, and *light*.**

Check to see that all students have filled in the correct answer space. Ask students if they have any questions.

SAY: **Now you will finish the test on your own. Read the directions carefully. Put your finger on number 1. Do numbers 1 through 21 just as we did S1. Read the questions and the answer choices carefully. Darken the circle for each correct answer. When you come to the words *GO ON* at the bottom of a page, continue working on the next page. When you come to the word *STOP* at the bottom of page 92, put your pencils down. You have 20 minutes to complete the test. You may now begin.**

Allow students 20 minutes to choose and mark their answers.

Test 9: Reference Materials

S1 A jacket
    B knee
    C its
    D light

STOP

For questions 1–21, darken the circle for the correct answer.

For questions 1–8, choose the word or name that would come <u>first</u> if the words in each group were put in alphabetical order.

1 A make
   B oar
   C party
   D napkin

2 J Powell, Bryan
   K Reyna, Andrés
   L Muenzler, Melissa
   M Nero, Jennifer

3 A tattoo
   B stuck
   C vote
   D uncle

4 J waddle
   K wall
   L wagon
   M waffle

5 A Royval, Tristan
   B Royal, Logan
   C Royster, Shu-Wei
   D Royce, Chauncy

6 J airline
   K aircraft
   L airplane
   M airfield

7 A Ruiz, Stephanie
   B Shaw, Shannon
   C Torrez, Yvette
   D Vara, Armando

8 J your
   K yard
   L yield
   M yell

GO ON
Level 9

89

Use the table of contents shown here to answer questions 9–12.

A Healthy World

Contents

9 Which chapter might tell about healthy snacks?

A Chapter 1

B Chapter 3

C Chapter 4

D Chapter 5

10 Which chapter might explain the steps to take in case of an accident or emergency?

J Chapter 1

K Chapter 3

L Chapter 5

M Chapter 6

11 Chapter 1 would tell you most about

A how to call 911.

B walking for exercise.

C ways to save the earth.

D catching a cold.

12 Where should you begin reading to find out about recycling newspapers so that we can use them again?

J Page 37

K Page 92

L Page 124

M Page 146

GO ON
Level 9

Use the dictionary and the pronunciation key shown here to answer questions 13–16.

Ss

sacred (sā´ • krid)
Deserving to be treated with great respect

salmon (sam´ • ən)
A kind of fish that is large
and has a silver body

A salmon

scribble (skrib´ • əl)
To write or draw quickly or carelessly

shatter (shat´ • ər)
To break into pieces

shed (shed)
To lose or drop

shrivel (shriv´ • əl)
To shrink, wrinkle, or wither

sofa (sō´ • fə)
A long seat that has a back and arms

A sofa

squash (skwosh)
A yellow or green vegetable
that grows on a vine

A squash

submit (səb • mit´)
To present

Pronunciation Key

a	at	o	hot	u̇	pull
ā	ape	ō	old	û	turn
ä	far	ô	song	ch	chin
â	care	ô	fork	ng	sing
e	end	oi	oil	sh	shop
ē	me	ou	out	th	thin
i	it	u	up	th	this
ī	ice	ū	use	hw	white
î	pierce	ü	rule	zh	treasure

The ə symbol stands for the unstressed vowel heard
in about, taken, pencil, lemon, and circus.

---

13 How should you spell the name of a kind of fish?

  A Selmon

  B Solmon

  C Salmon

  D Sulmon

14 Which word fits best in the sentence "He had scribbled so much on his paper that he was embarrassed to _____ it"?

  J submit

  K shatter

  L shrivel

  M shed

15 The *a* in *shatter* sounds like the *a* in

  A sofa.

  B sacred.

  C salmon.

  D squash.

16 What might you do to a plate?

  J Shatter it

  K Scribble it

  L Shrivel it

  M Submit it

GO ON
Level 9

91

This card catalog contains author, title, and subject cards that are arranged alphabetically. Use the card catalog to answer questions 17–18.

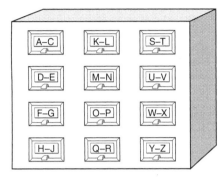

17 Which of the drawers should you use to find joke books by Chris Thomas Mattingly?

  A Drawer A–C

  B Drawer H–J

  C Drawer M–N

  D Drawer S–T

18 Which of the drawers should you use to find books about when dinosaurs lived and why they disappeared?

  J Drawer D–E

  K Drawer H–J

  L Drawer K–L

  M Drawer W–X

For questions 19–21, choose the best place to find the information.

19 Where in a book should you look to find a list of difficult words and their meanings?

  A In the index

  B In the glossary

  C On the title page

  D In the table of contents

20 Which of these would you find in a dictionary?

  J A story about how to use an anchor

  K Poems about anchors

  L The pronunciation of the word *anchor*

  M Directions for making an anchor

21 Which section of the library would have stories that are not true?

  A Fiction

  B Gardening

  C Sports

  D Biography

STOP
Level 9

92

SAY: **It is now time to stop. You have completed Test 9. Make sure you have carefully filled in your answer spaces and have completely erased any stray marks. Then put your pencils down and close your books.**

After the test has been scored, review the questions and answer choices with students. If students are having difficulty, provide them with additional practice.

TEACHER NOTES

TEACHER NOTES

TEACHER NOTES